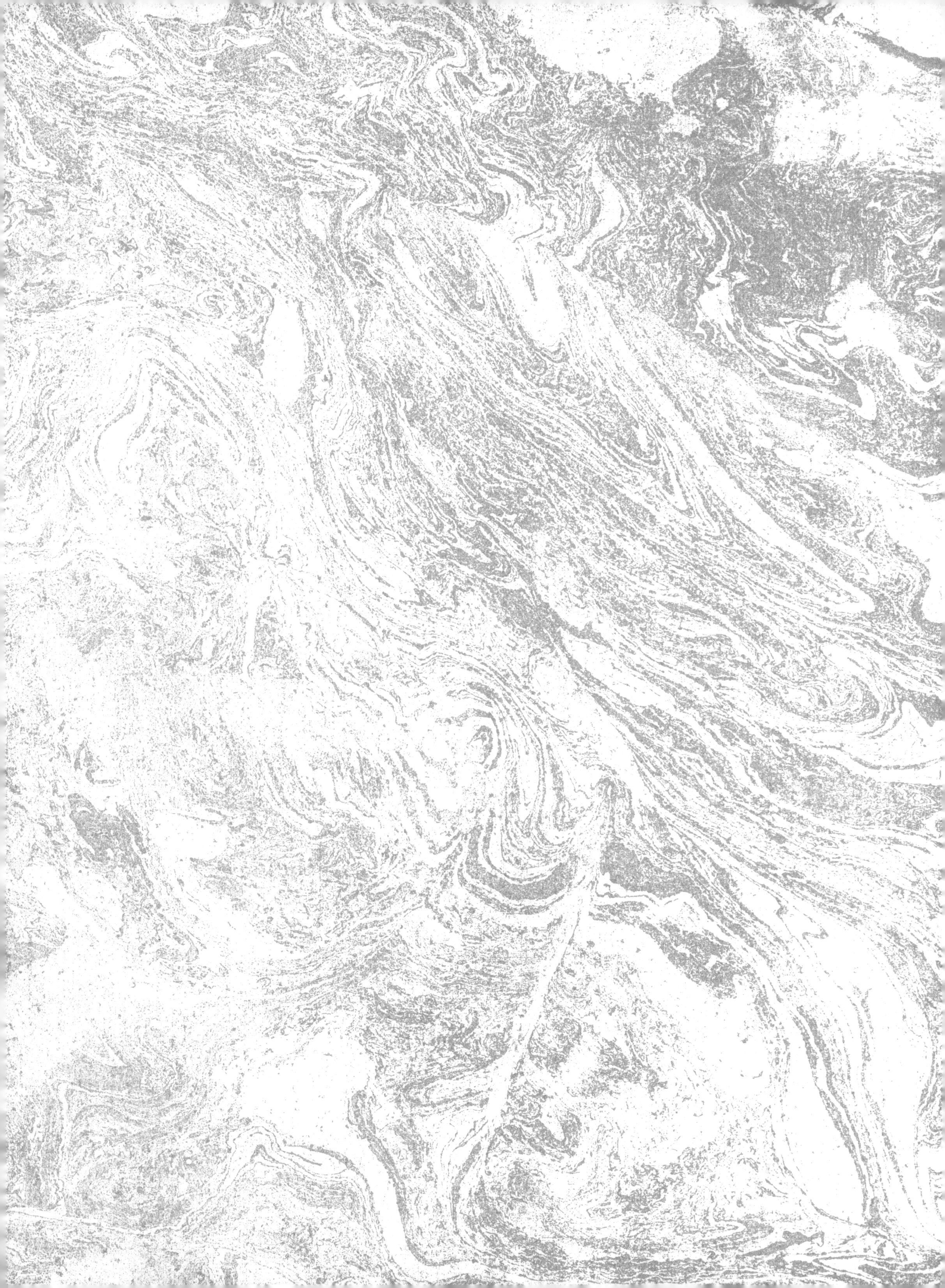

方解石

郷司基晴写真集

Calcite
MOTOHARU GOUSHI

Calcite

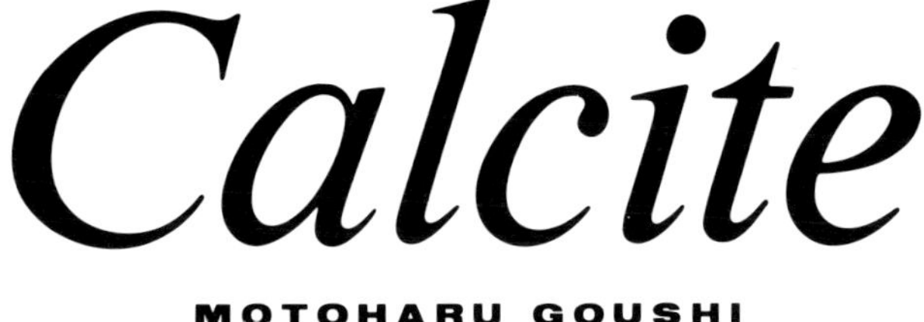

MOTOHARU GOUSHI

TREVILLE

郷司基晴はかつて私の大学の教え子であった。私が直接に手とり足をとっての授業はなかったが、彼は他の学生とは明らかに異なる髪形や服装をしていたものの、そんなことよりもその頃からすでに自らの独自な世界を探究しようとしていたことが強く印象に残っている。郷司基晴は大学で毎年行なうフォックス・タルボット賞というコンクールに入賞した。入賞作品はキラリと光るものがあり、すぐれた写真家の片鱗を見せていた。

そして年を経て次に見せられたのがこゝにある作品群であった。私はふとメイプルソープを連想したが、それは私の間違いというもので、郷司基晴の写真は、もっと過激で危険な美の秘部に入り込んでいる。

エロチシズムの探究は人間存在を探るもっとも困難で深淵な道であると思われるが、郷司基晴は敢然とその困難に挑み、身をもって自らの裸身をさらして彼岸の絶壁から深淵の迷路に身を投じたのである。暗い混沌の中での葛藤はどれほど辛らく苦しいものであったろう。彼岸のこちら側にいる私などには分る術もないが、ようやく郷司基晴という若い写真家の戦慄にも似た無気味さを知らされたのである。

これは正にいまの日本における貴重な鉱脈の発見であり、おゝいに祝福されなければならない。

序文

細江英公

Motoharu Goushi was a student of mine at the university where I teach. I didn't interact much with him in the class, but I do remember him as being quite different from the other students in his hair style and clothes. He gave me the strong impression that he was already trying to find his own unique world. While at school, Motoharu Goushi won the Fox Talbot Prize given at an annual contest. Even then, his work provided a glimpse of his immense telent as a photographer.

Now, years later, I have been shown these pictures. Momentarily, this work reminded me of Mapplethorpe but now I realize I was mistaken. The photography of Motoharu Goushi enters into the secret aspect of violence and shows its dangerous beauty.

The study of eroticism is perhaps the deepest and most difficult path to an understanding of human existence. Motoharu Goushi has fearlessly confronted its difficulties. He stripped himself naked and then leapt boldly into a deep maze. His struggle in that dark confusion must have been excruciating. As I stand outside of the maze, my only clue to the intensity of the conflict is the shivering that the eeriness of this young photographer's work induces.

Like the discovery of a precious mine of diamond, Goushi's work should be openly celebrated in today's Japan.

Foreword
by Eikoh Hosoe

なぜものにはかたちがあるのか。

そのことについて、ギリシア神話も、旧約聖書も、四福音書も、どんな説明もしてくれない。誰もがどんな説明もしてくれないなら、自分で考えてみるほかないだろう。

もののかたち、たとえば薔薇の莟でもいい、筋肉の組識でもいい、それを美しいと見る時、私たちはその美しさがやがて崩れ、腐敗し、溶け去り、ついには無くなってしまうことを知っている。無くなることを知っているがゆえに、いっそう美しい、と思う。

ここから理解されることは、ものにかたちがあるのは、そのかたちがいずれ解体され、そのものじたいがやがて無に帰するためらしい、ということだ。どうやら私たちは、いずれ解体しやがて無に帰するそのゆえにこそ、もののかたちに強く惹きつけられるものらしい。

とすれば、私たちの欲情する目は窮極的には解体に、腐敗に、無の闇に激しく誘惑されていることになる。じつは翻ってほかならぬ私たちの欲情する目も解体し腐敗し無化すると知った時、私たちはカメラ・オブスクーラなる装置を発明した。

カメラ・オブスクーラなる欲情の装置の意味は、フォルムという無の仮象の永遠化という見果てぬ夢の機械である。この見果てぬ夢の機械はそれじたい誘惑者となって欲情する目を手招きする。わが郷司基晴の作品はことごとく恍惚と不安とに痙攣していることによって、彼が選ばれた犠牲者であることを証明している。

フォルムの誘惑

高橋睦郎

Why does a thing have a shape?

Neither the mythology of the Greeks, nor the Old Testament, nor the four Gospels provide an answer to this question. Since no one seems able to explain it, I have no choice but to try to understand it for myself.

When we see the shape of an object, for example, a rose bud or a human physique, we see it as beautiful. But we also know its beauty will soon collapse, decay, and finally, vanish. Indeed, we think its form even more lovely because we know it will quickly be gone.

What I perceive from this is that the shape of a thing contains the dynamic of its dissolution and ultimate non-existence. We tend to be strongly attracted to the shape of something because we foresee its collapse and eventual disappearance.

Our hungering eyes are violently seduced by dissolution, decay, and ultimately, by the darkness of nothingness. In fact, after we realized that our living eyes themselves would also die and cease to exist, we invented the camera obscura.

The original purpose of equipment such as the camera obscura was to externalize our unfinished dreams, to show the temporary shape of ultimate nothingness. But then the products of the machine themselves began to seduce us and to beckon our passionate eyes. Motoharu Goushi's work here proves that he is a chosen victim of their allure, captured in a spasm of ecstasy and anxiety.

The Temptation of Shape
by Mutsuo Takahashi

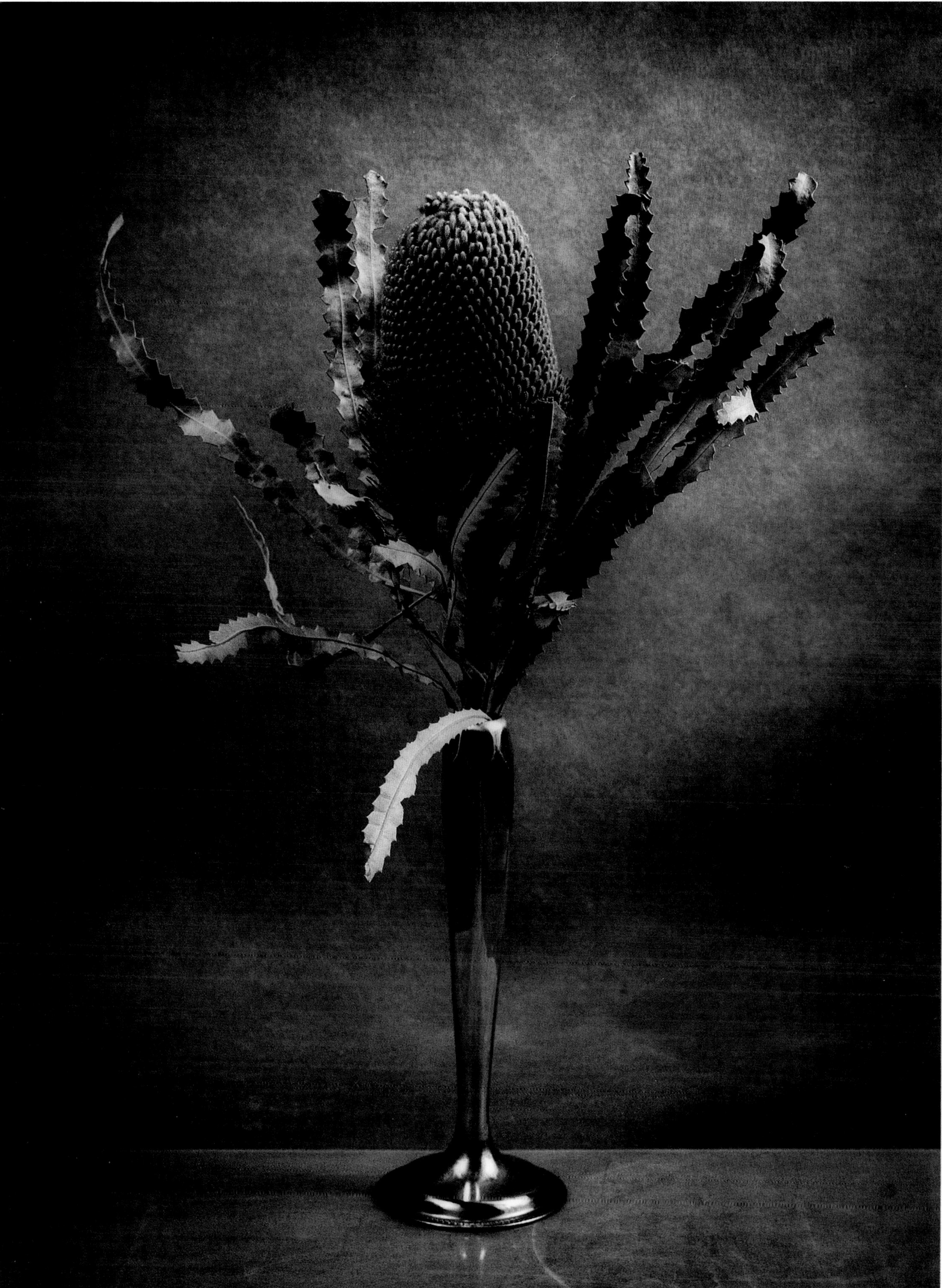

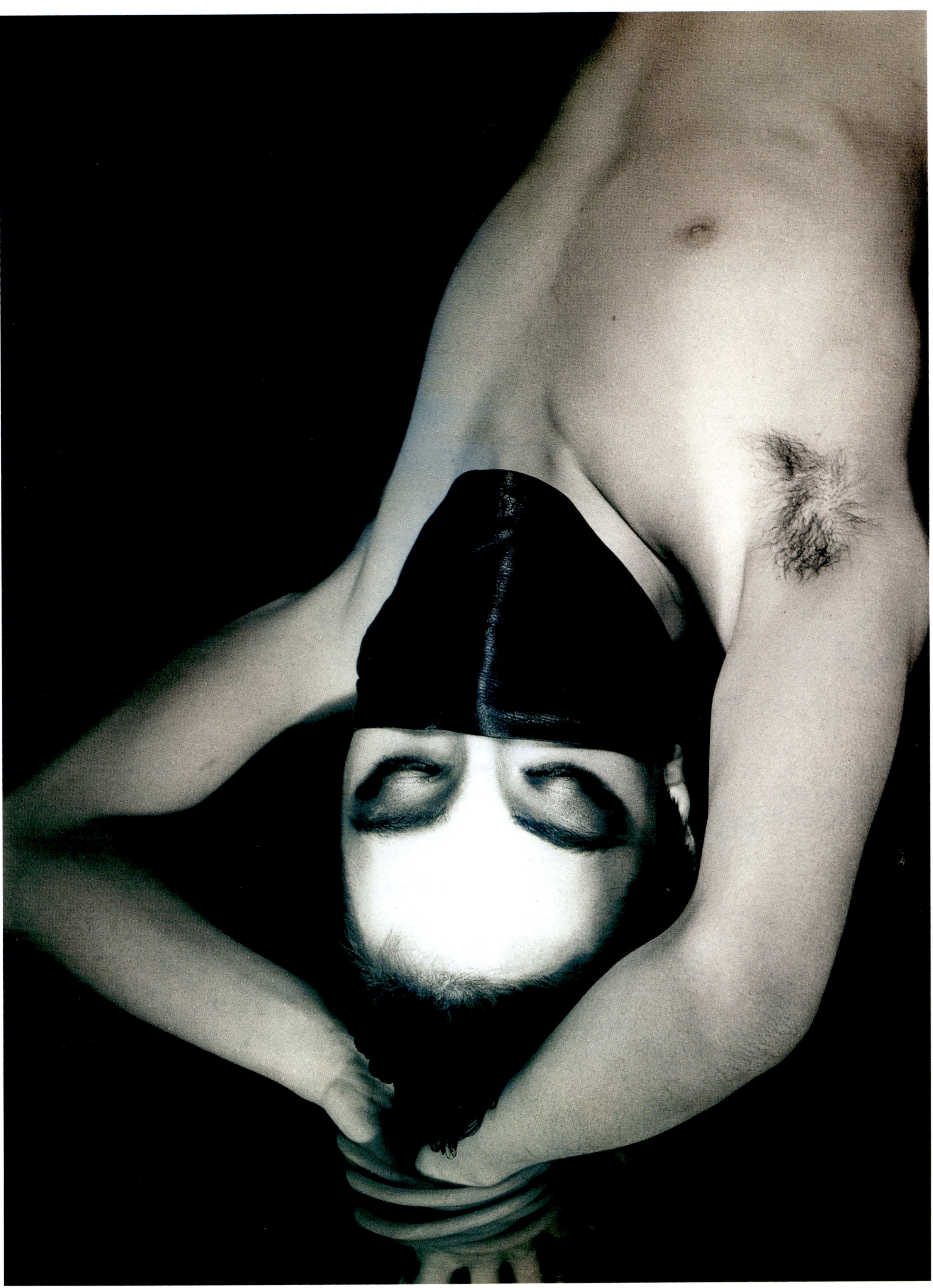

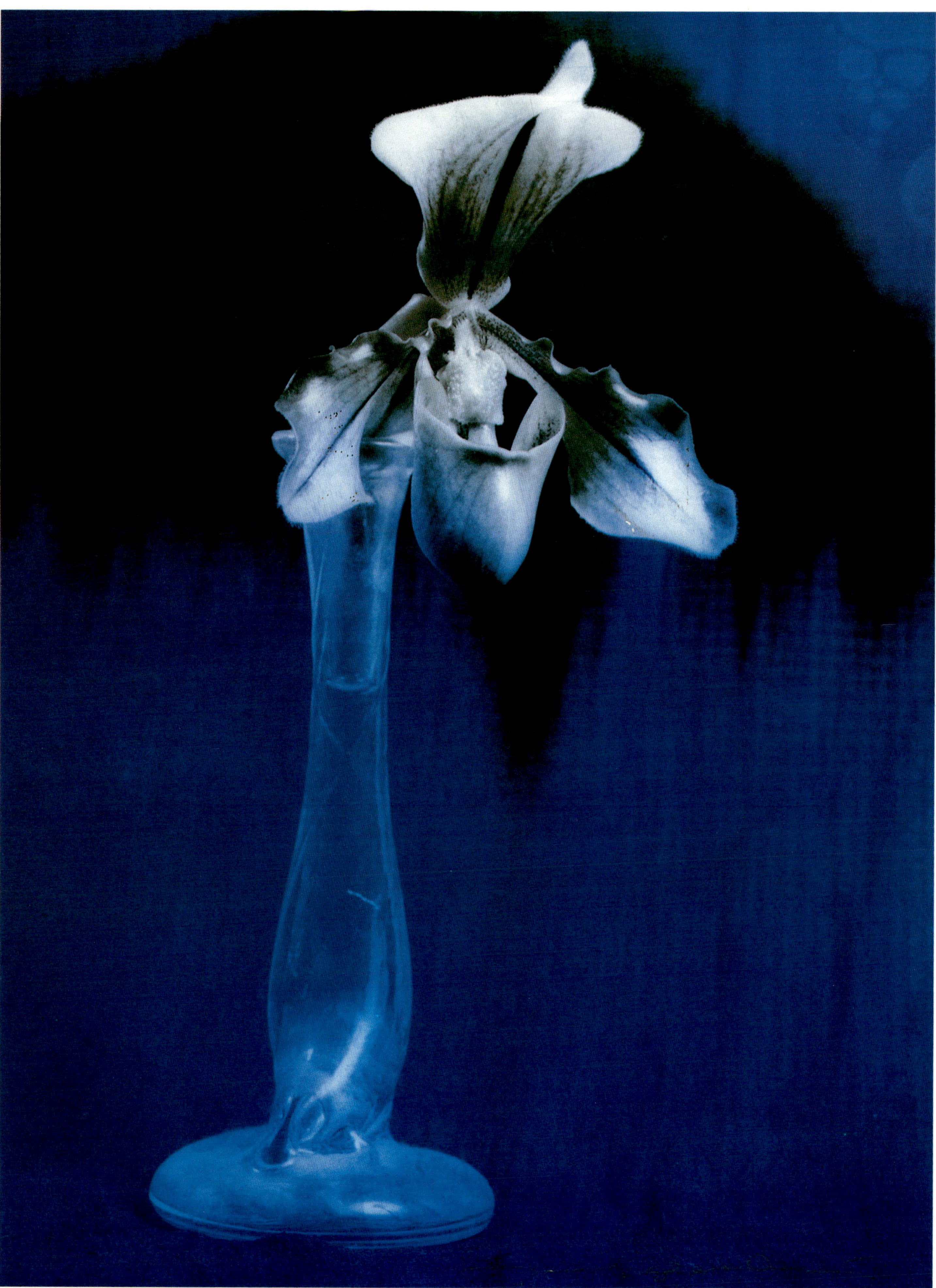

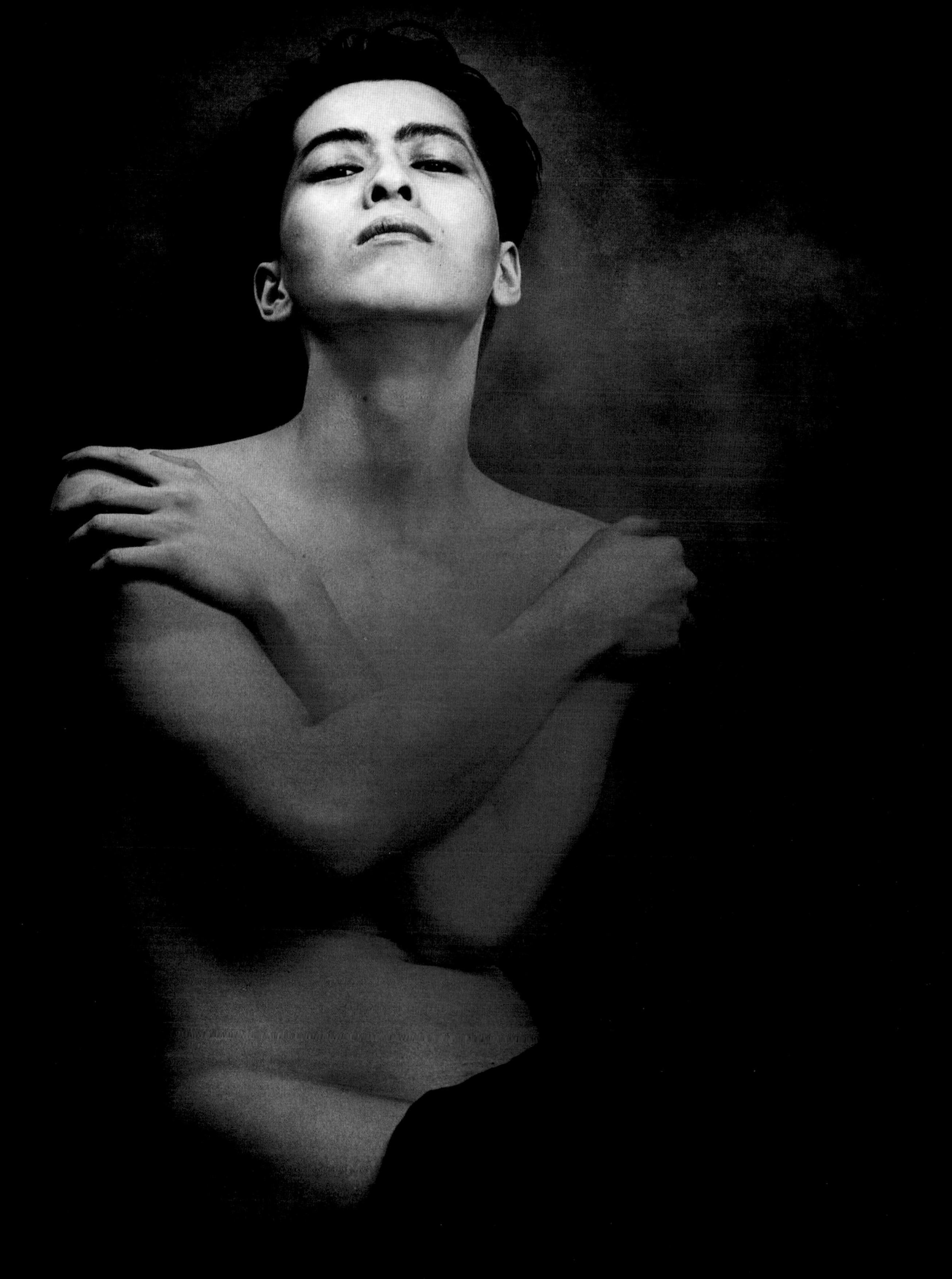

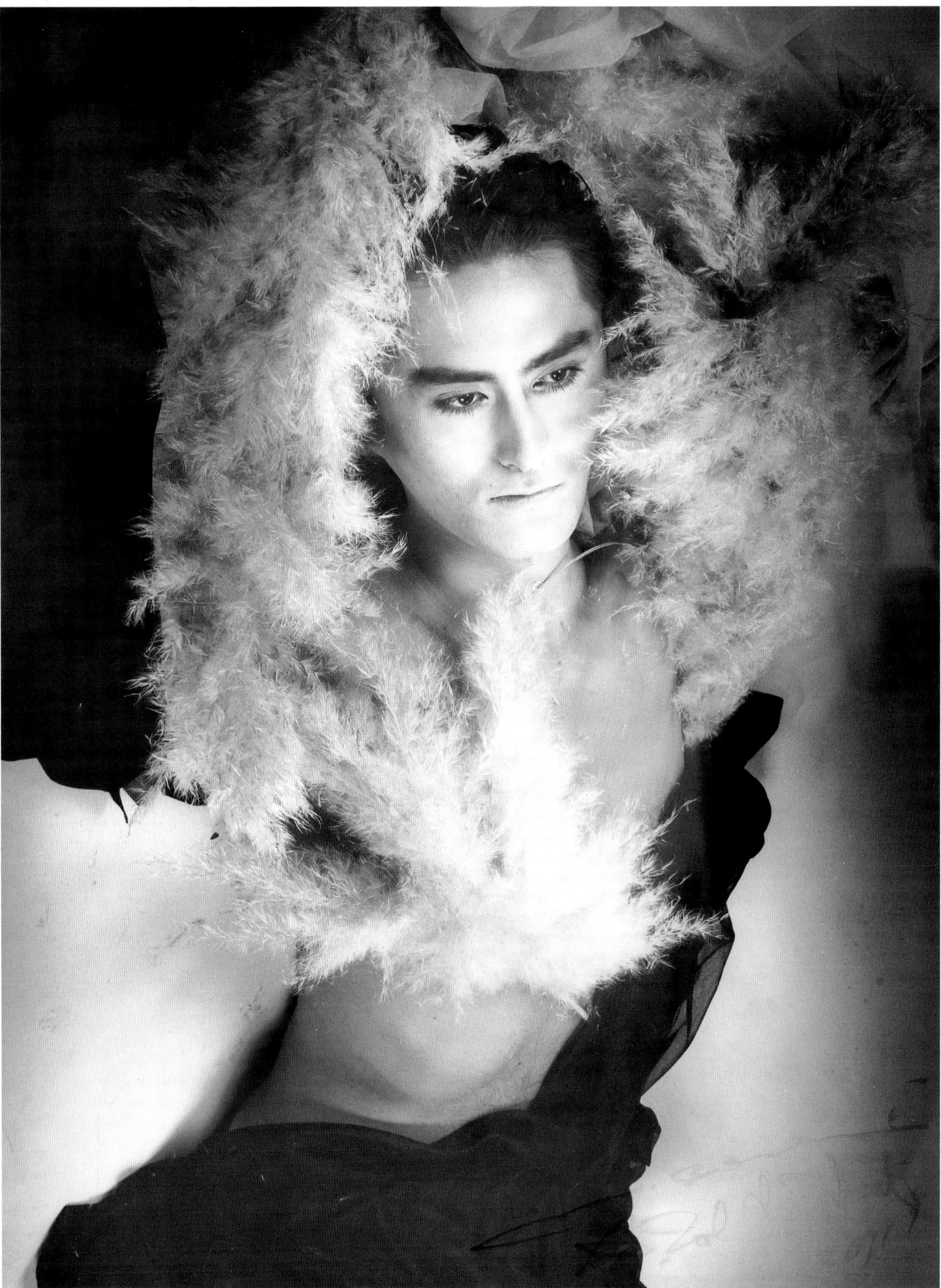

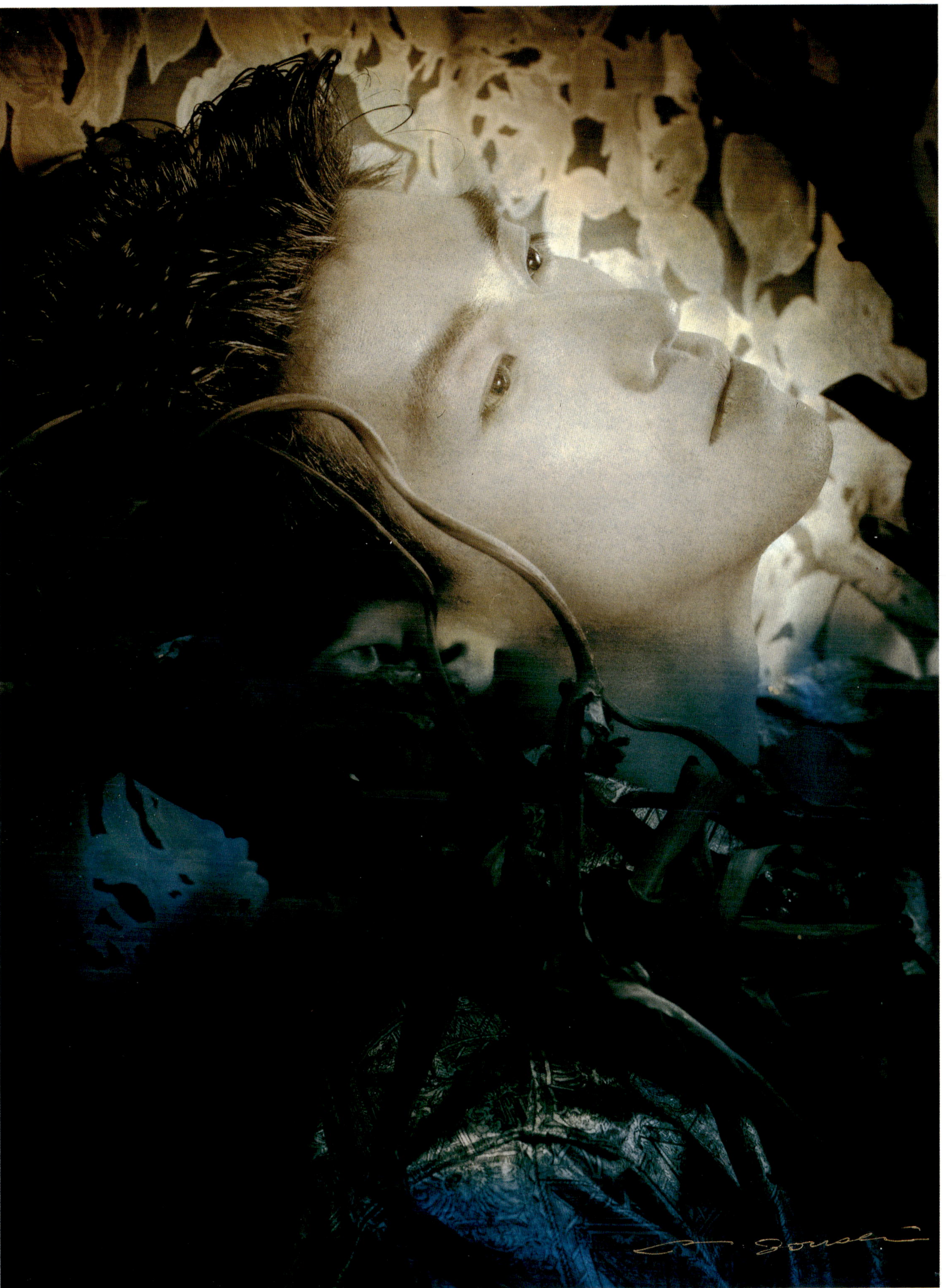

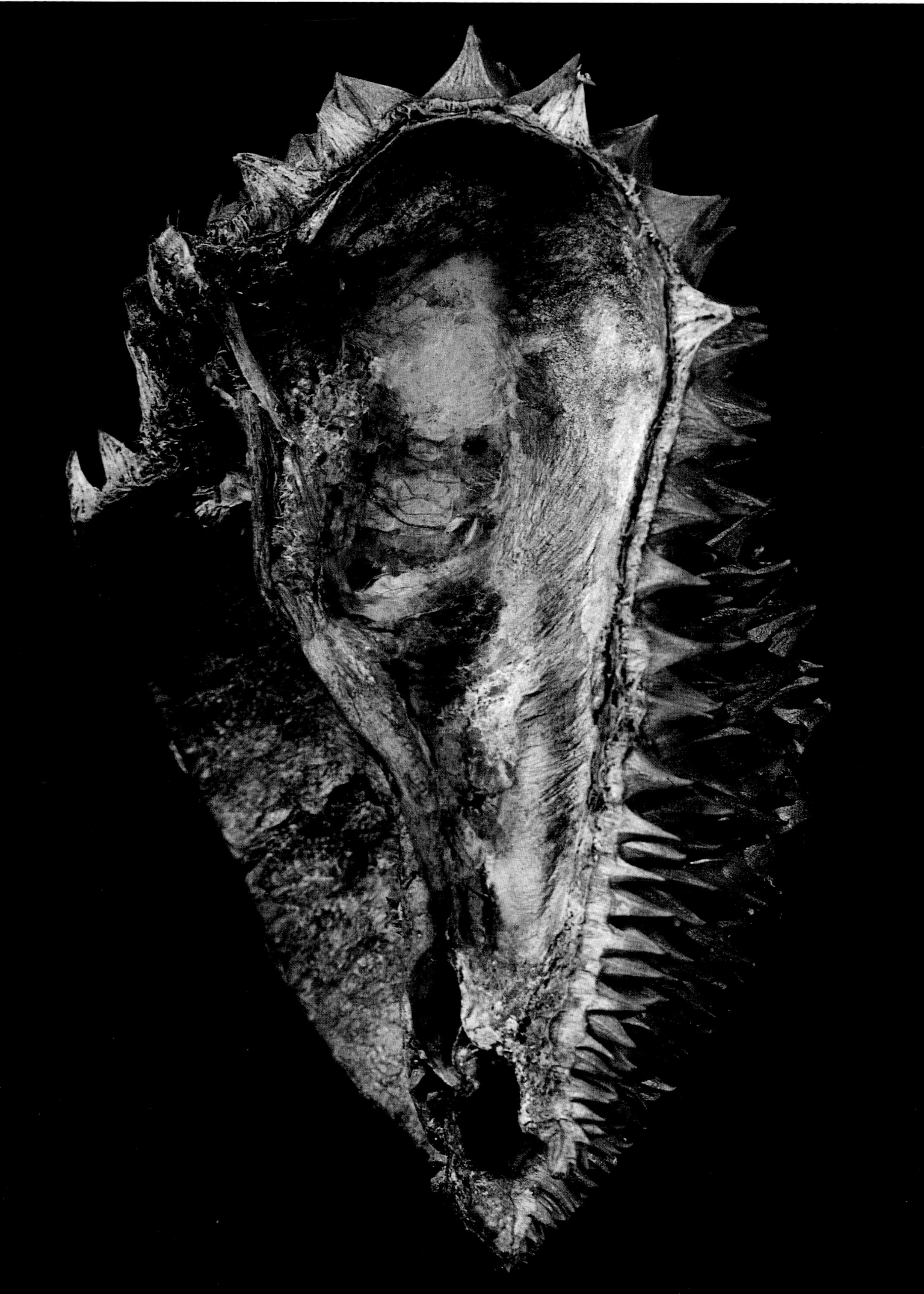

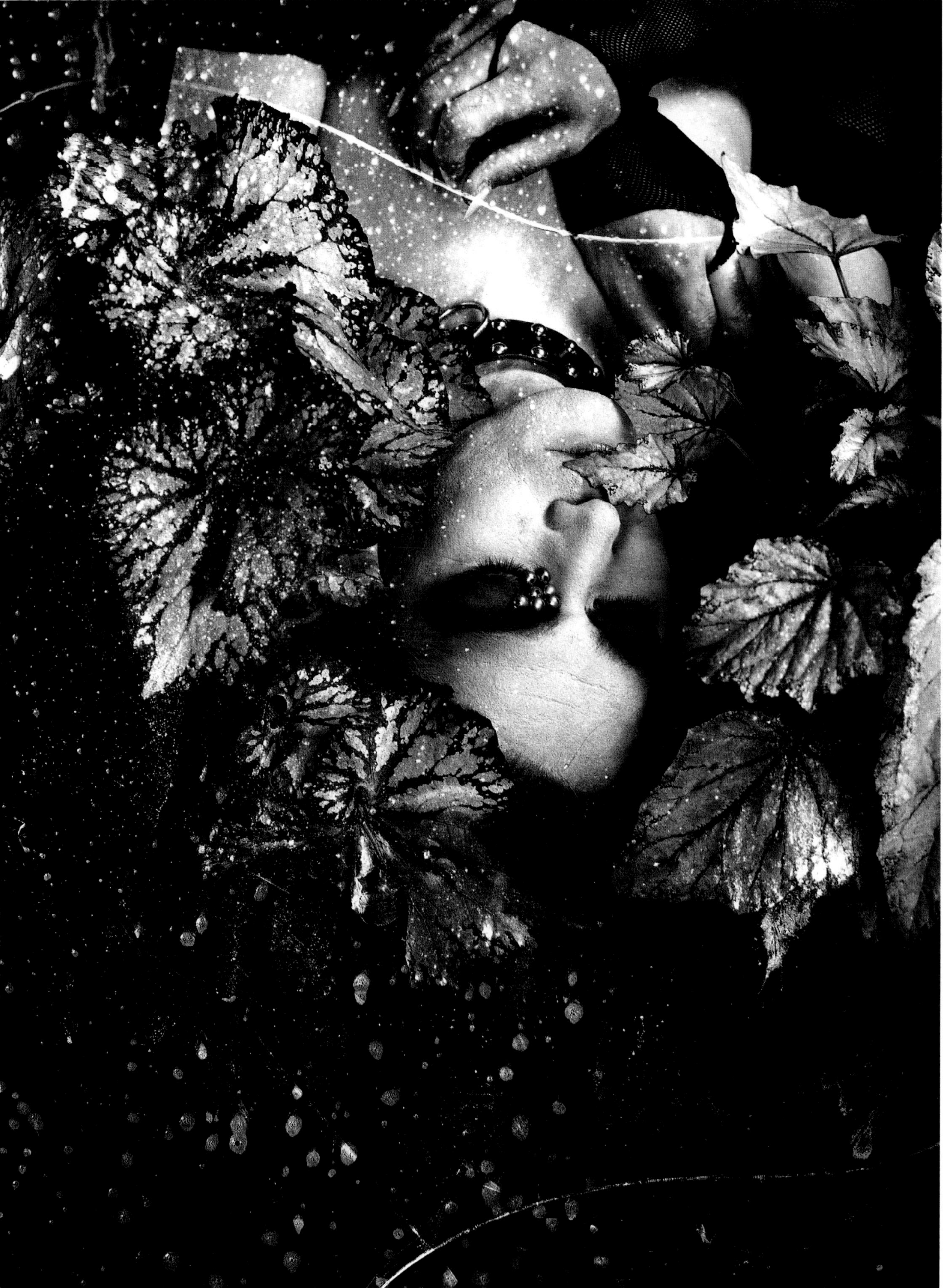

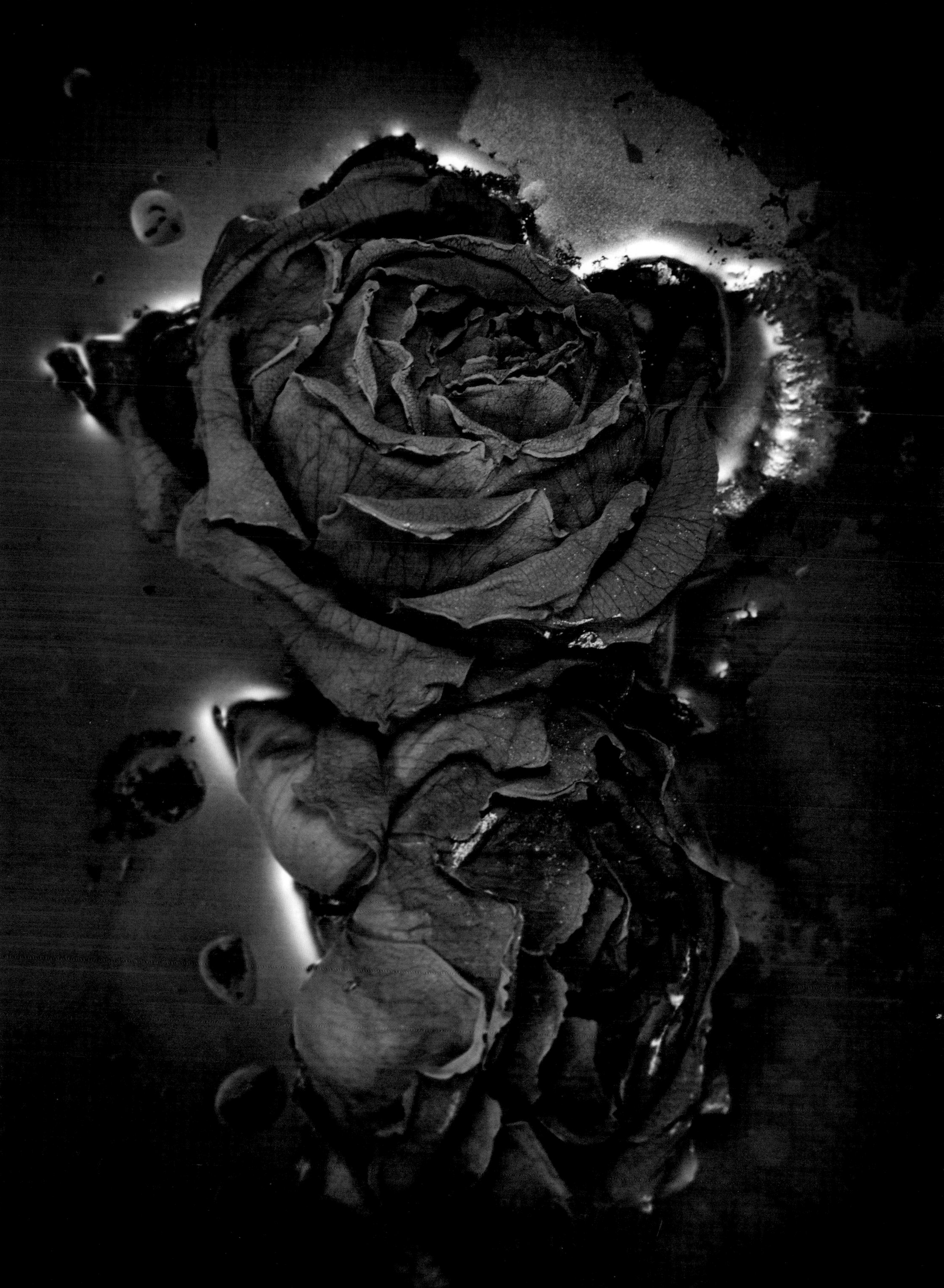

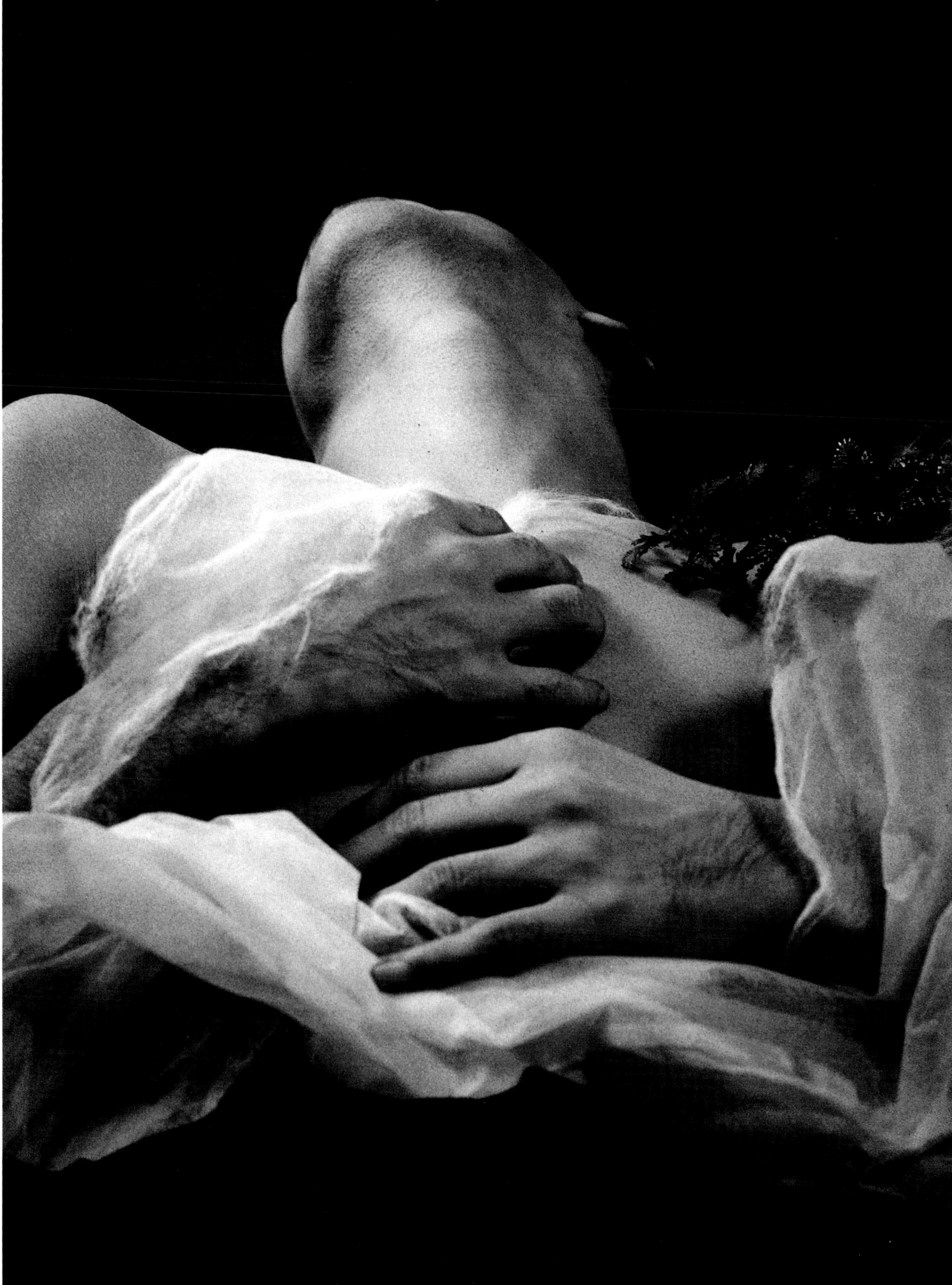

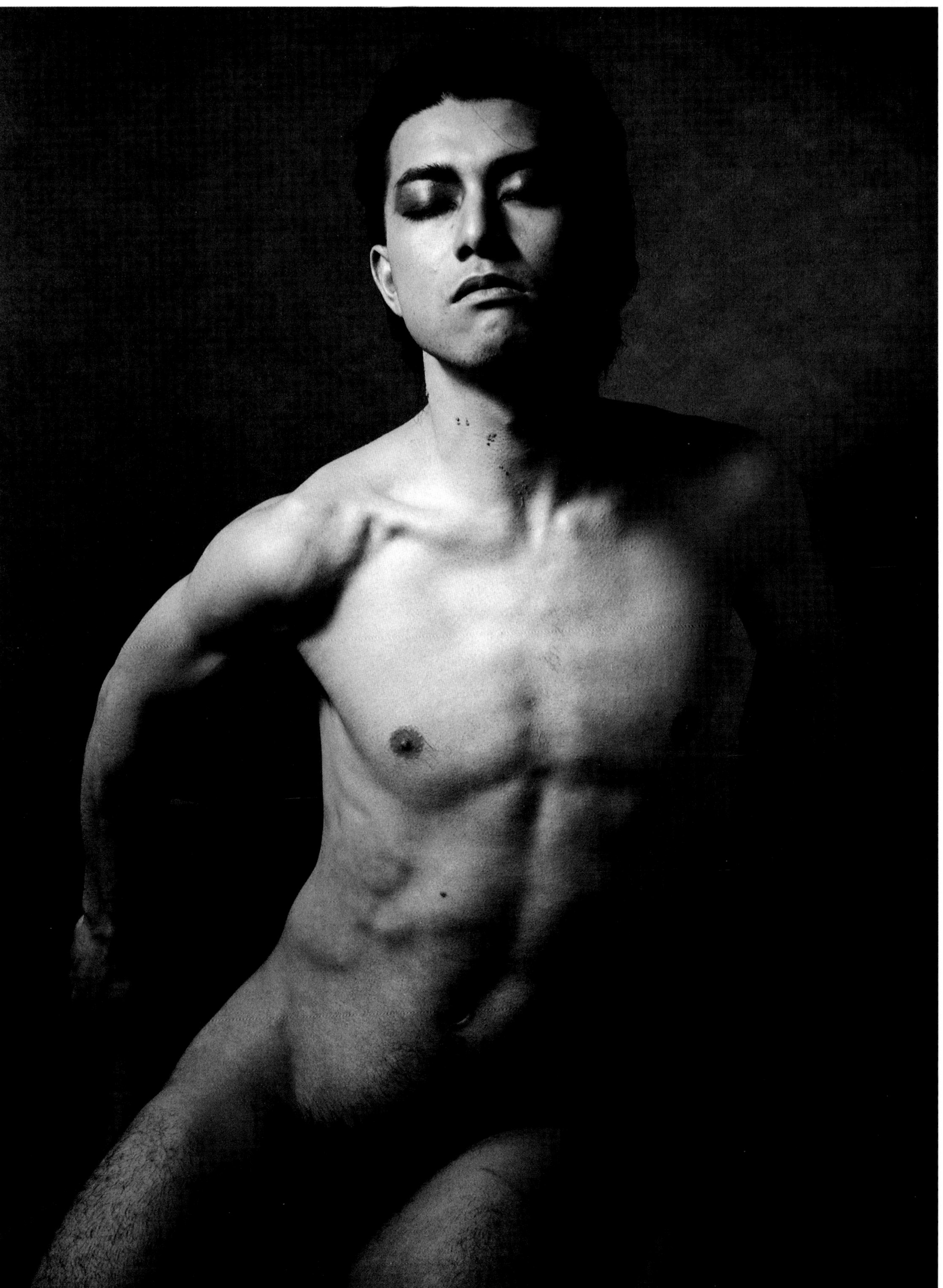

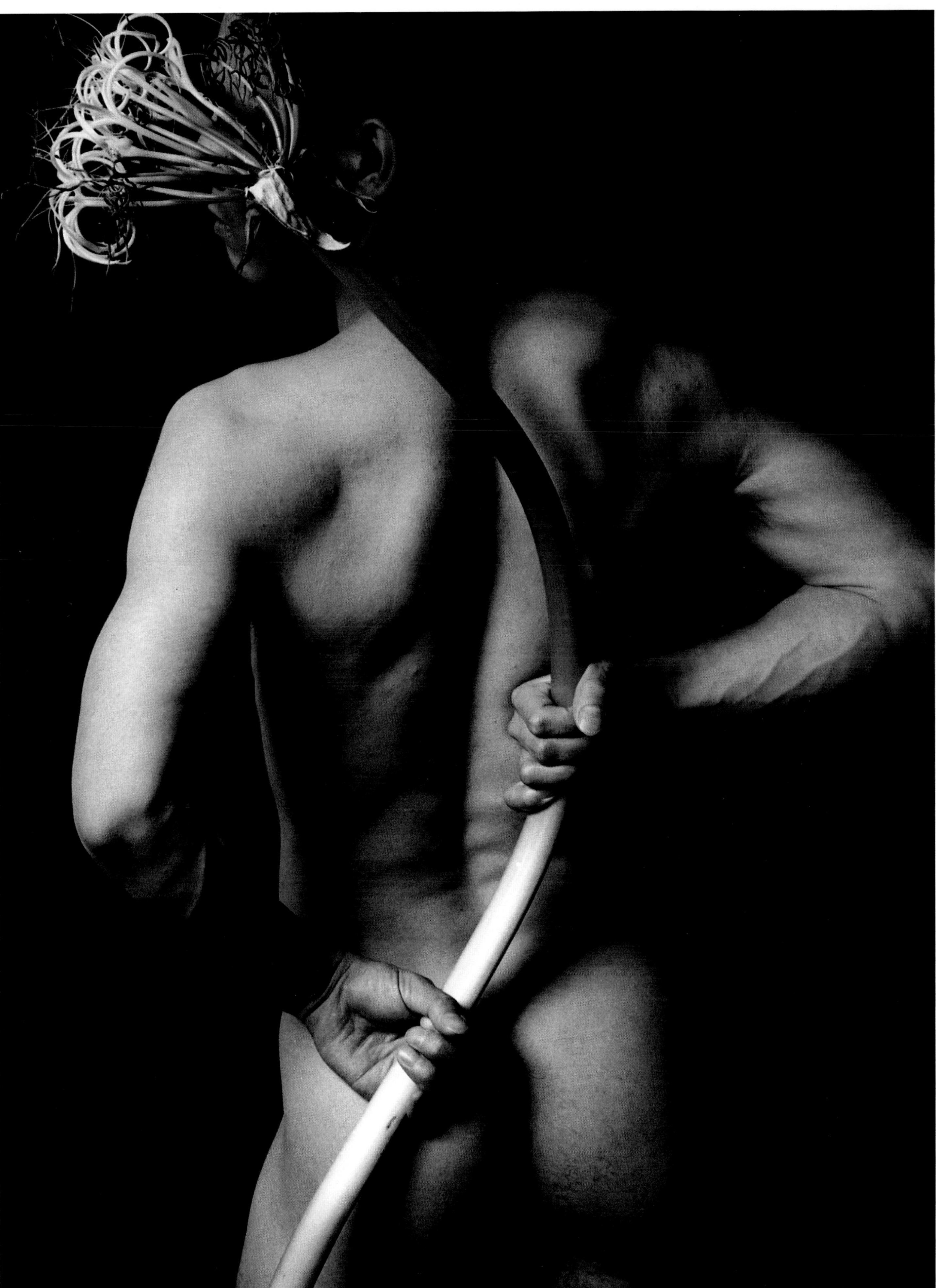

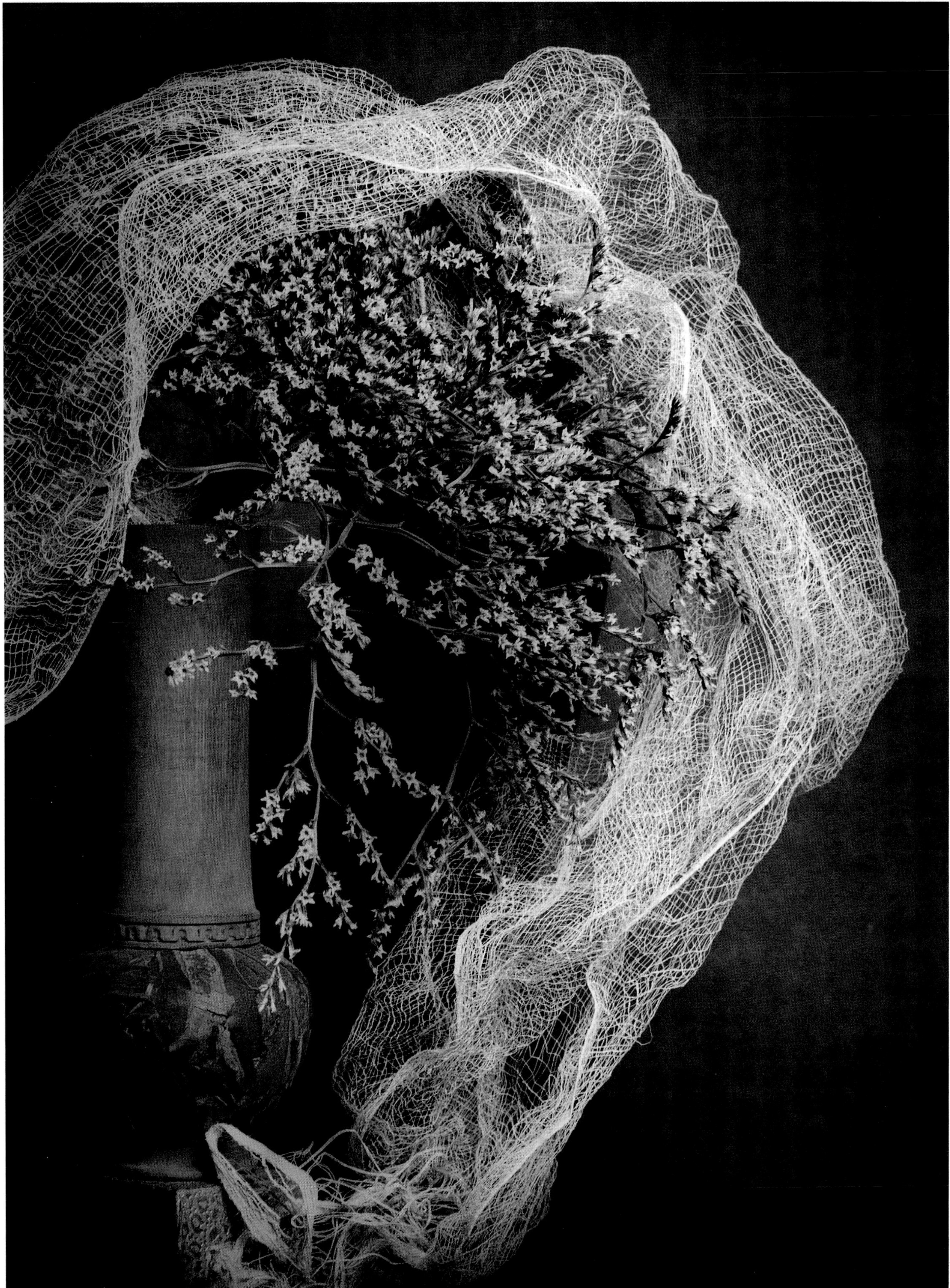

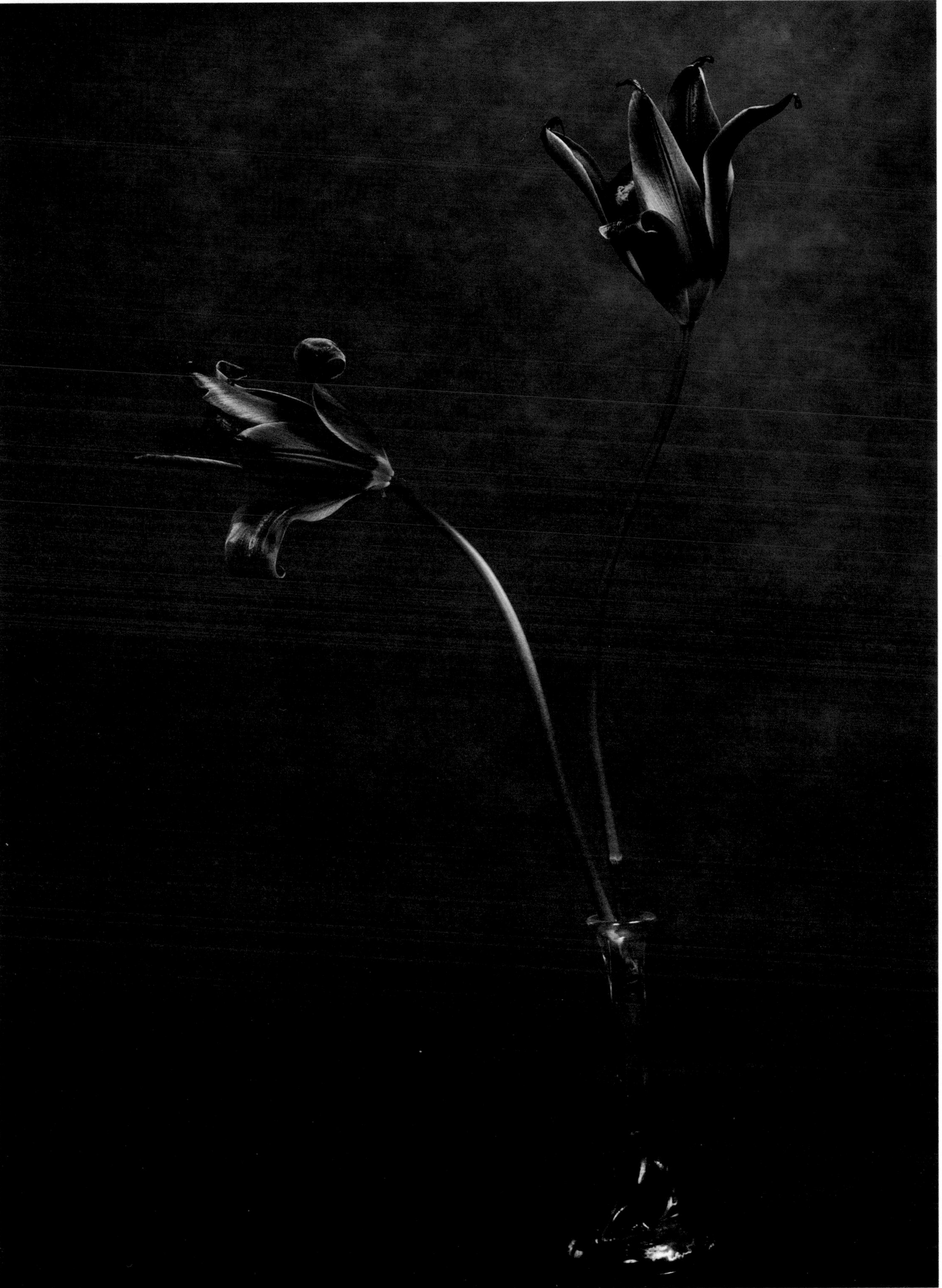

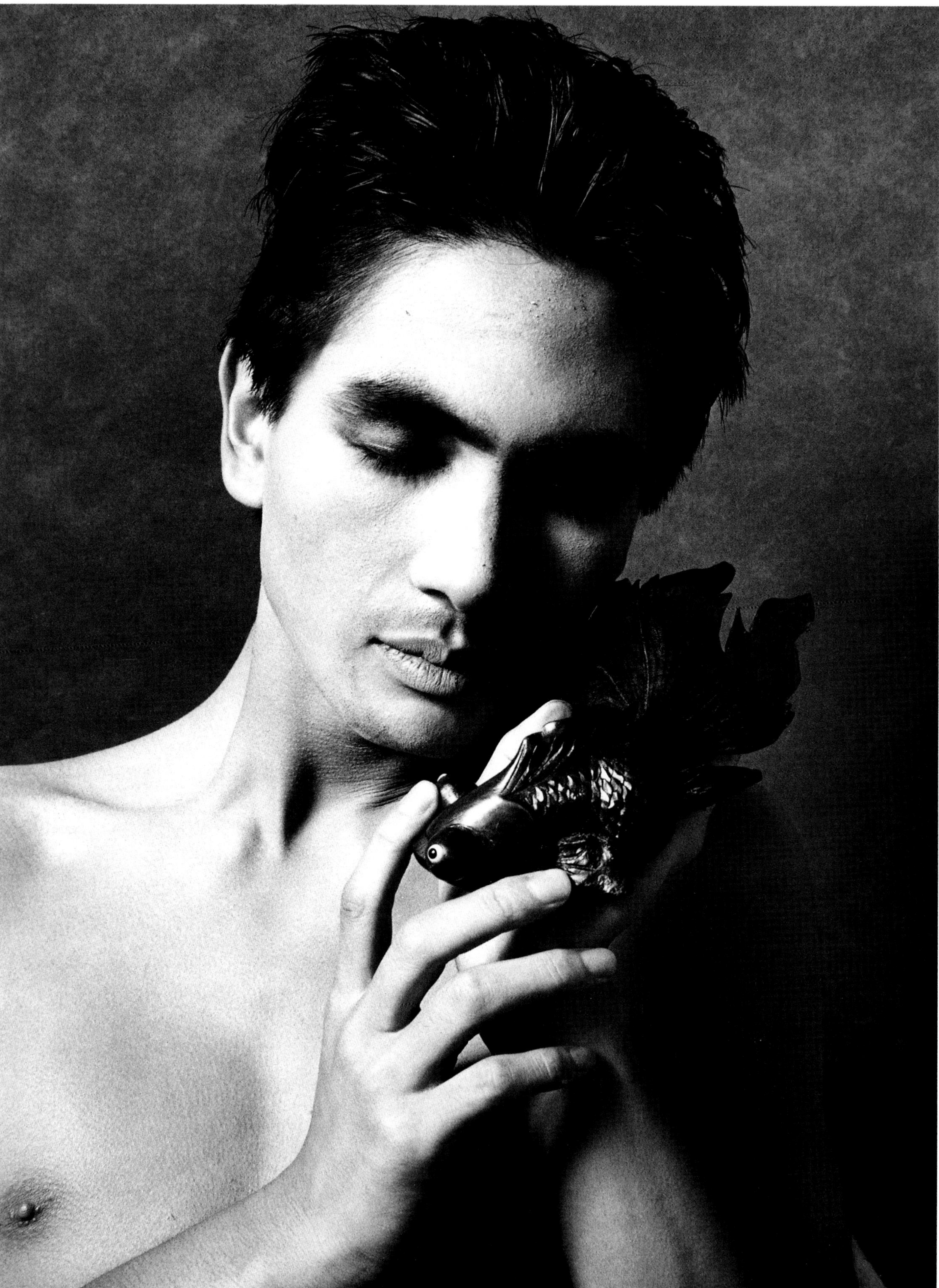

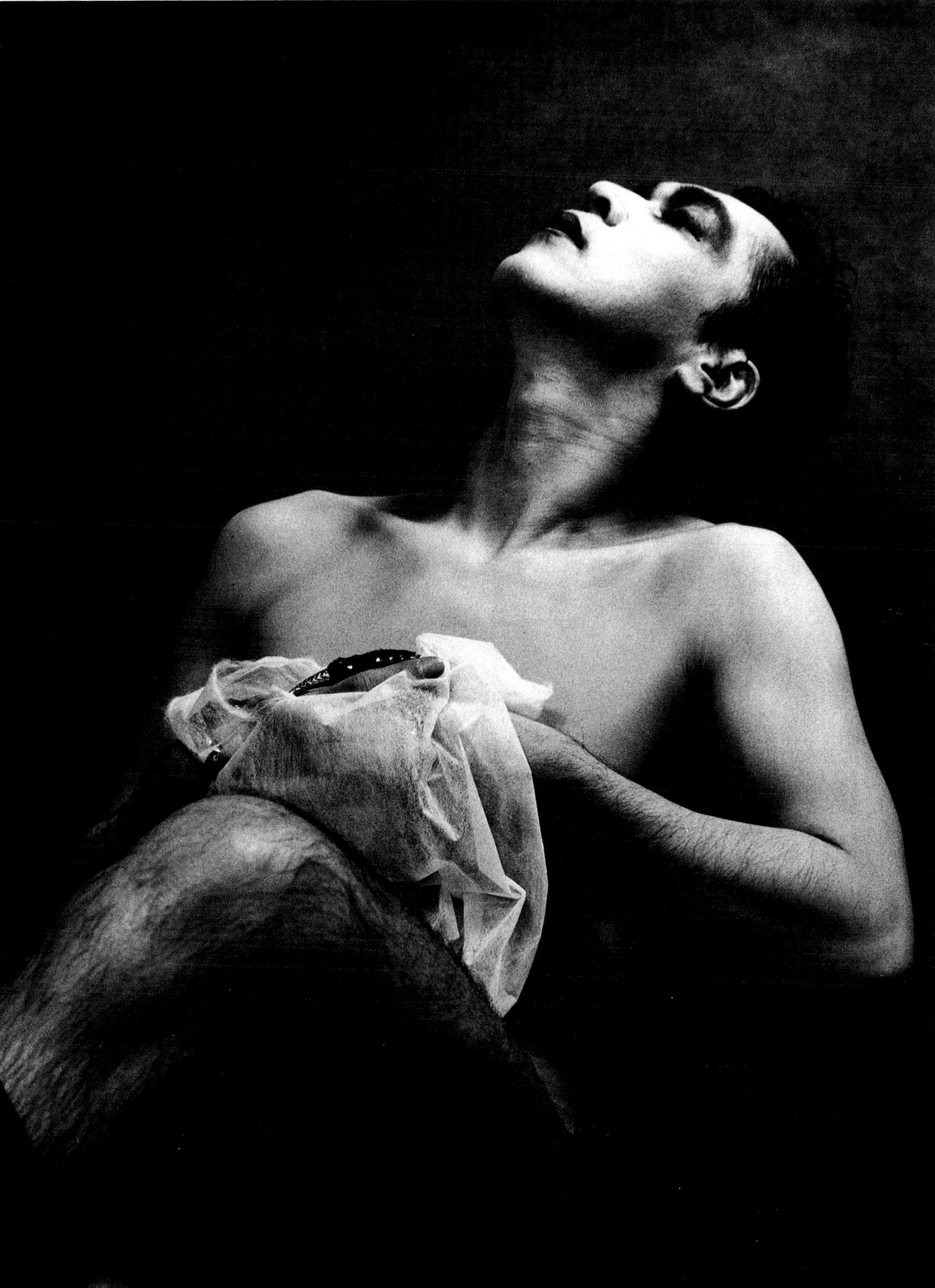

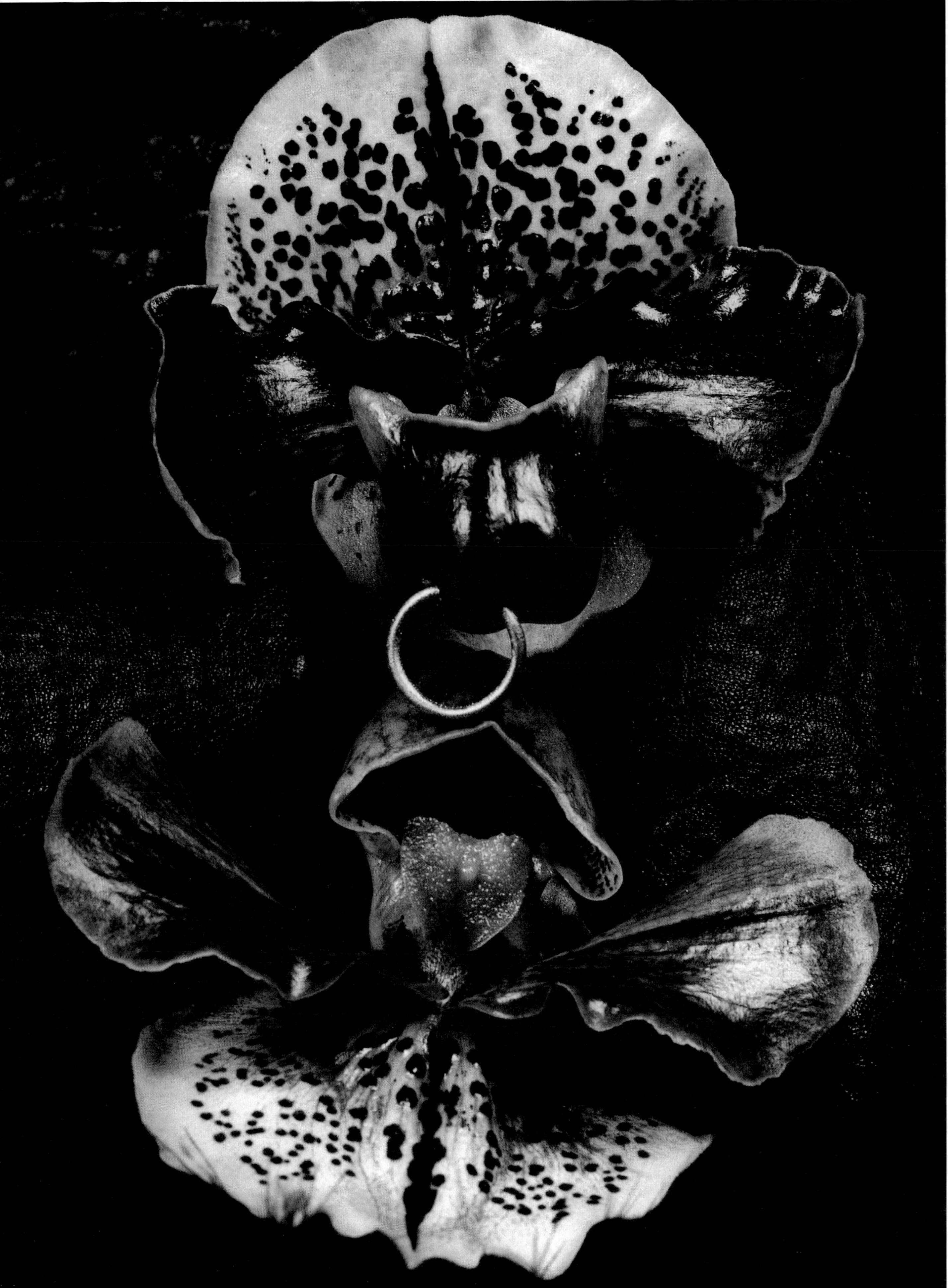

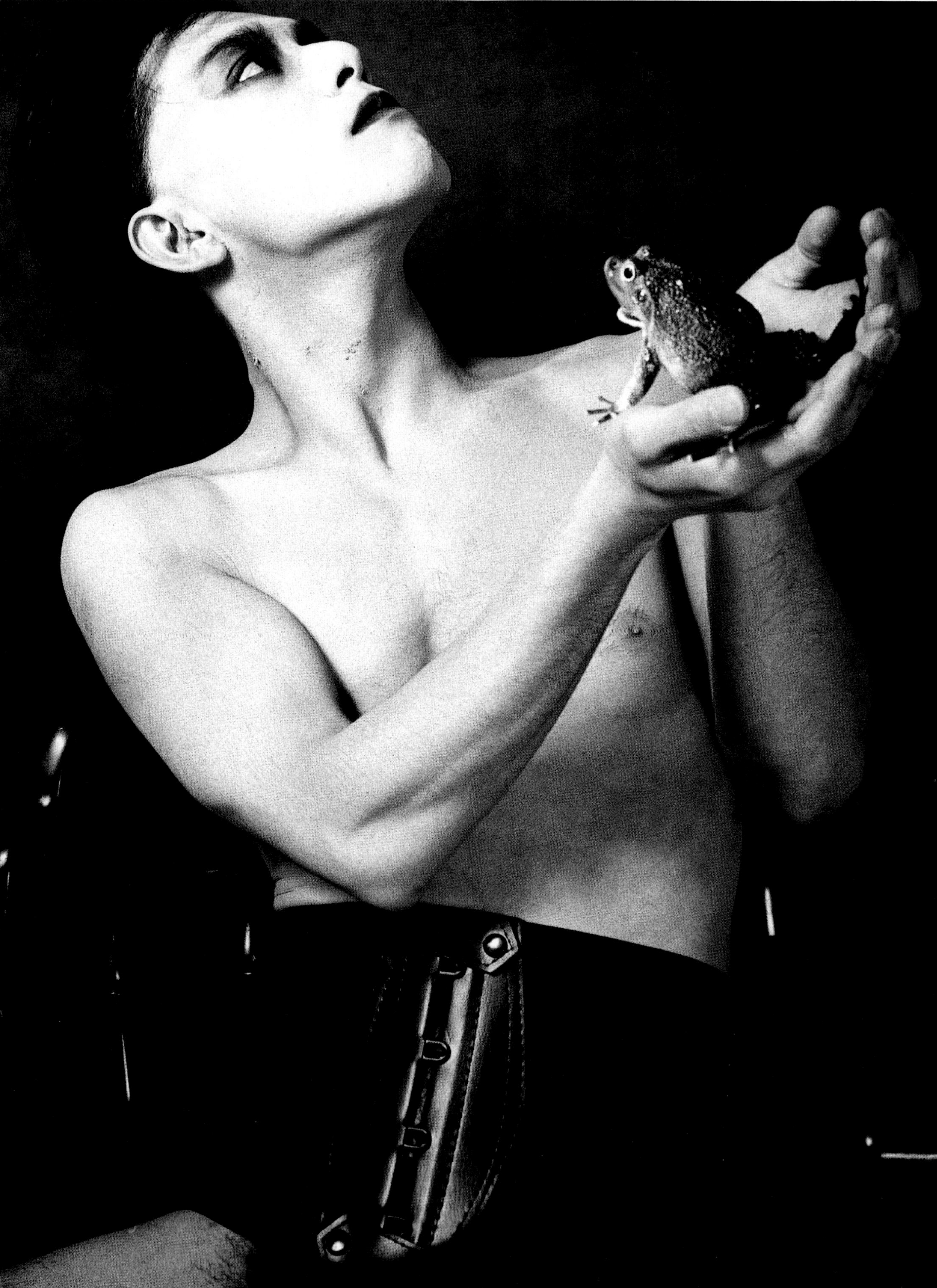

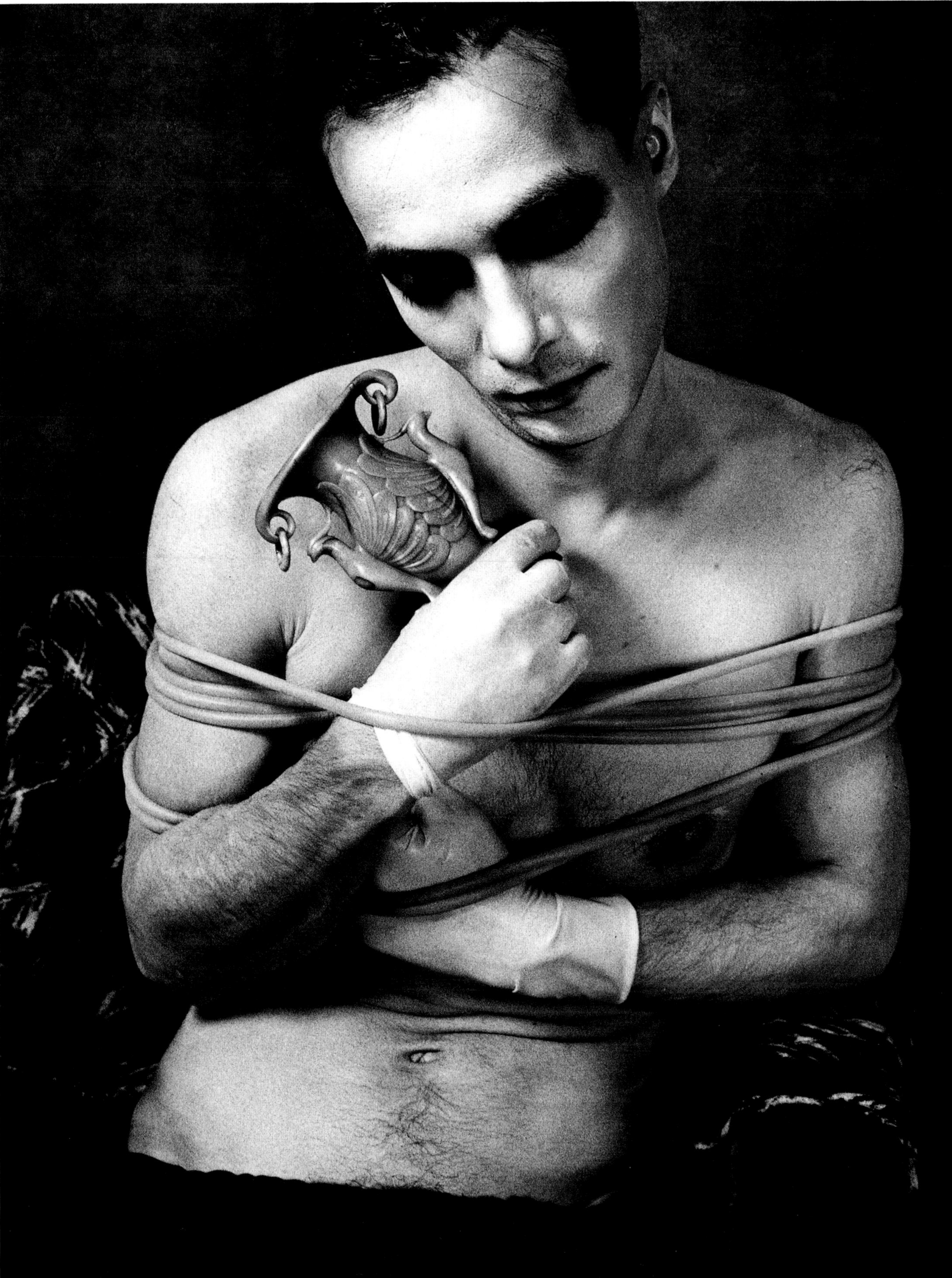

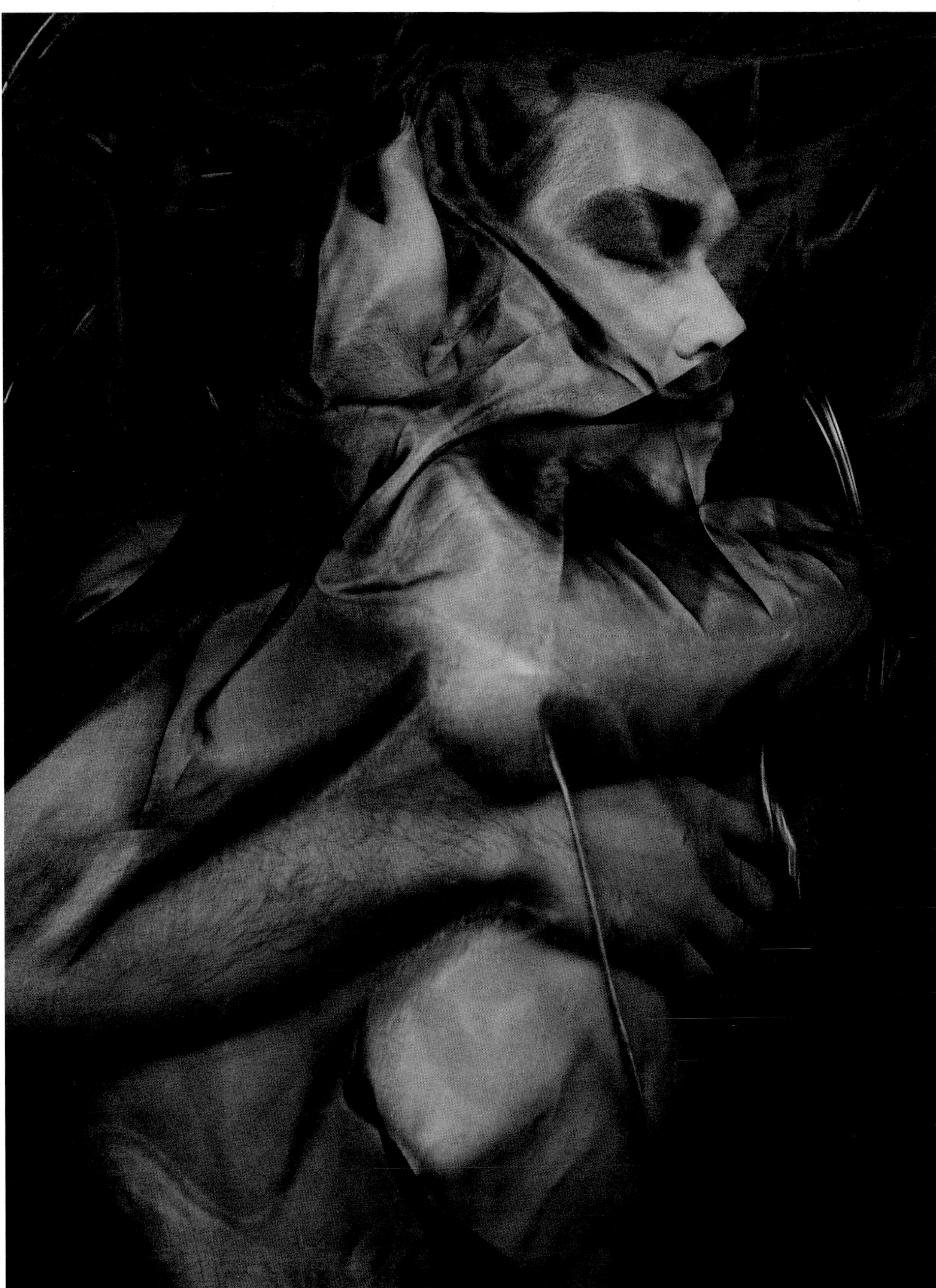

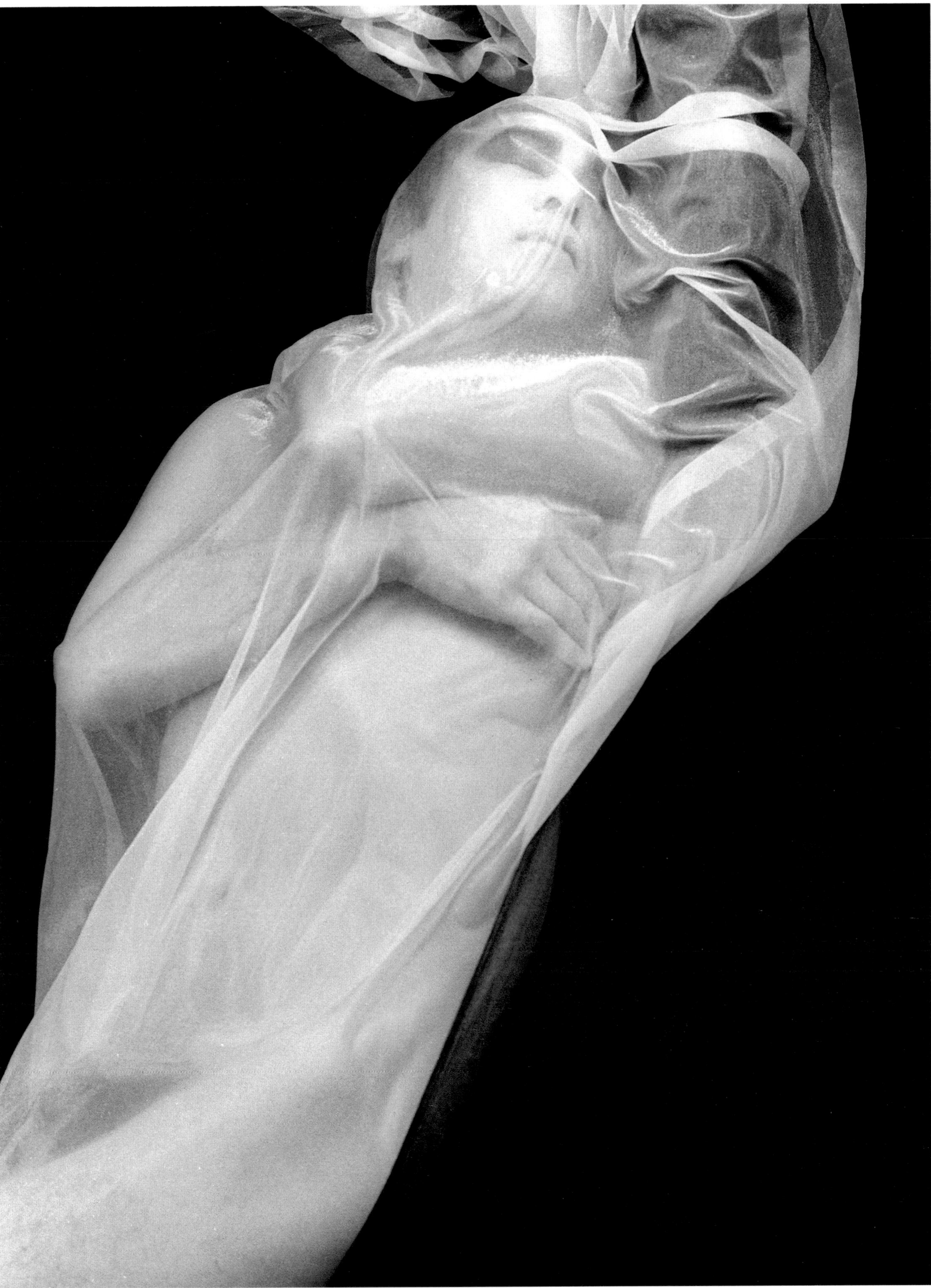

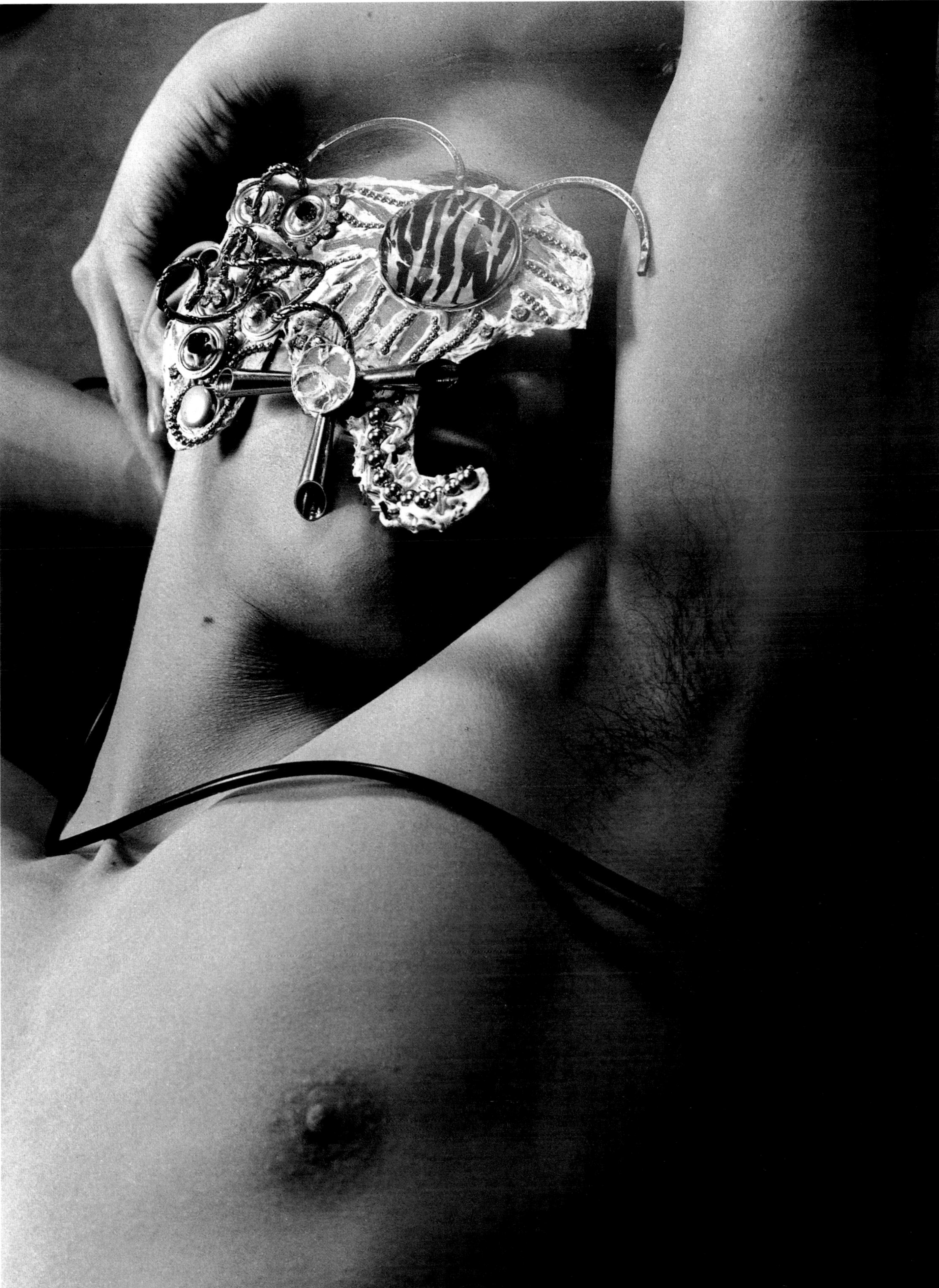

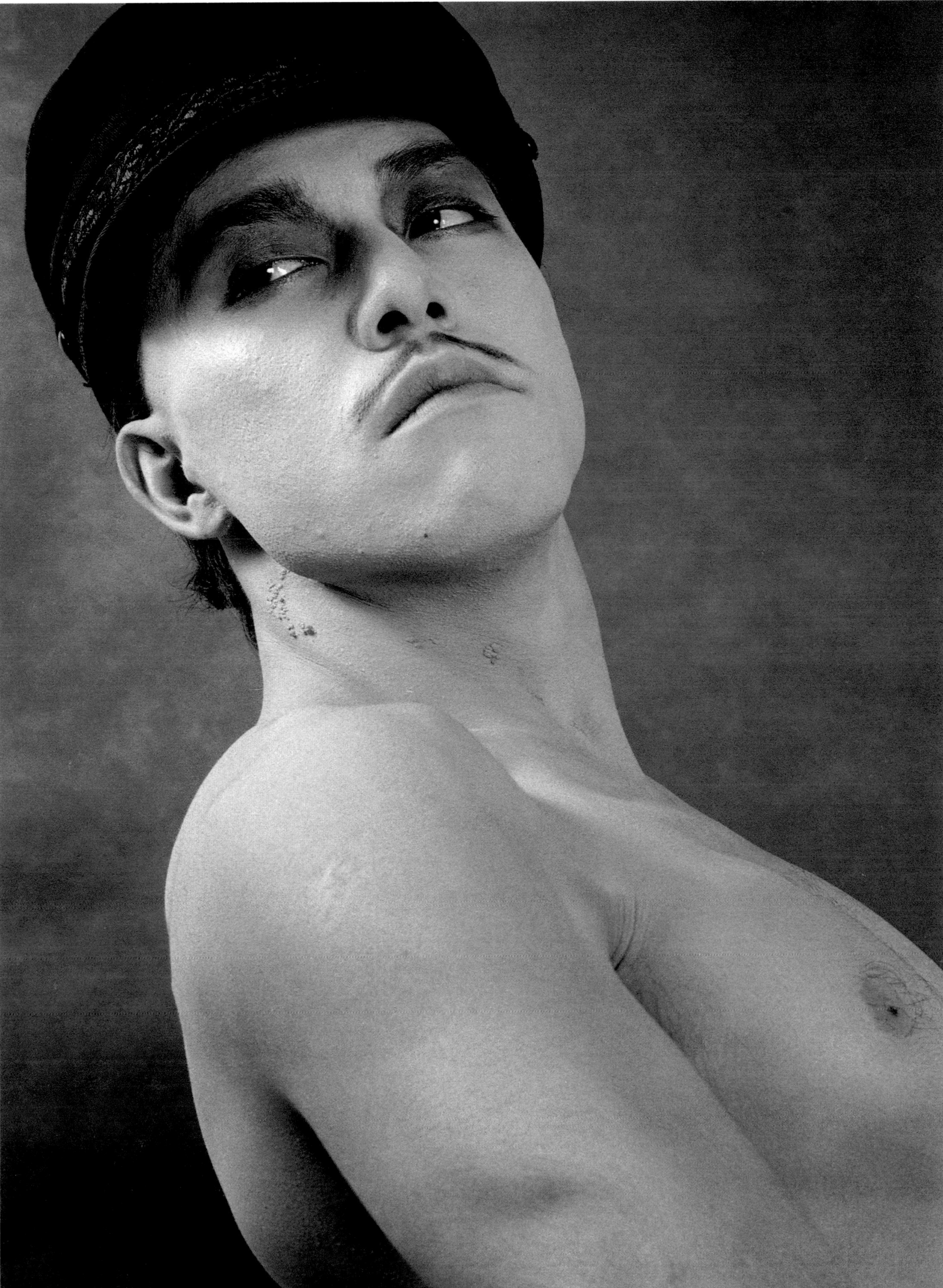

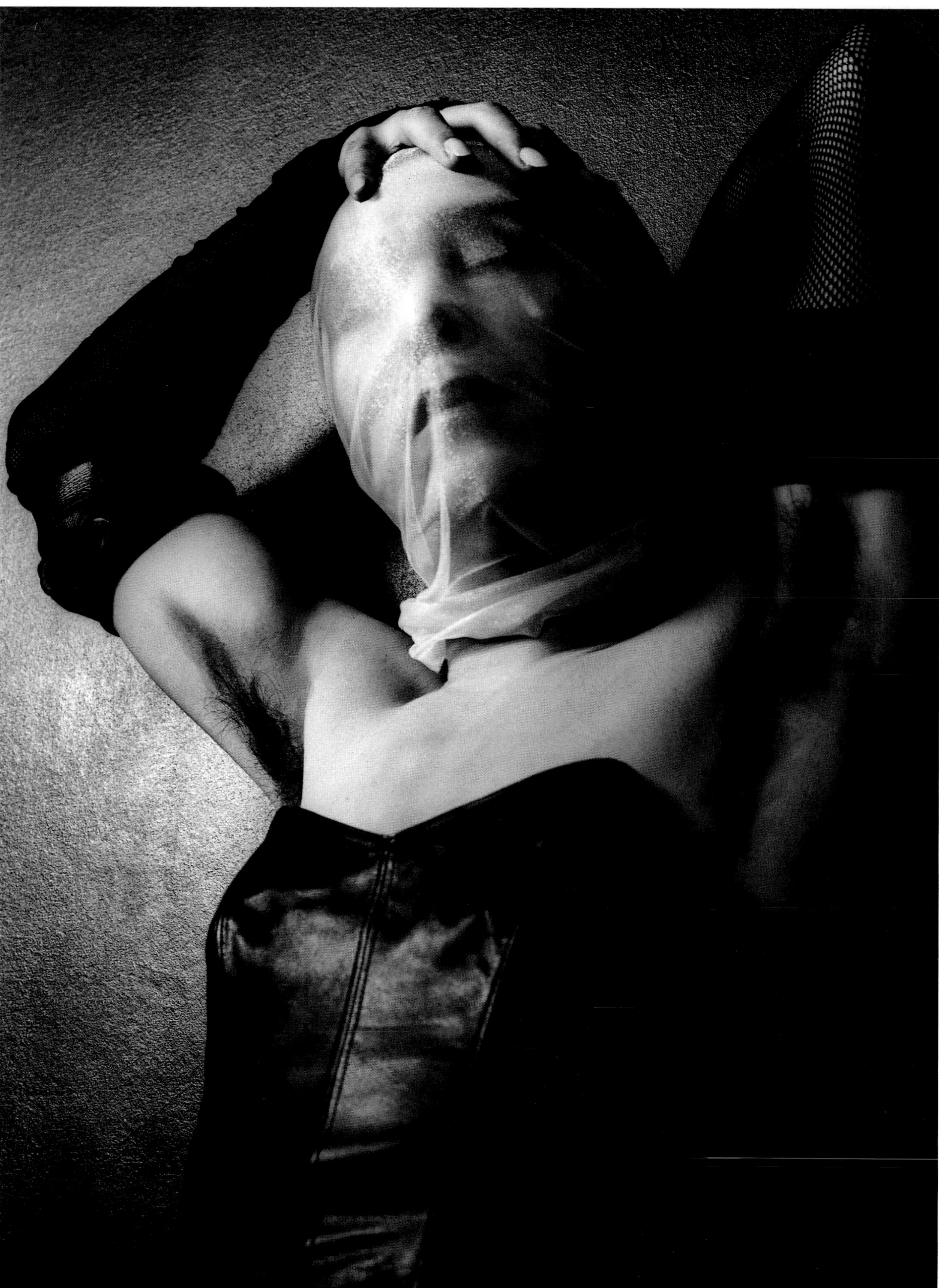

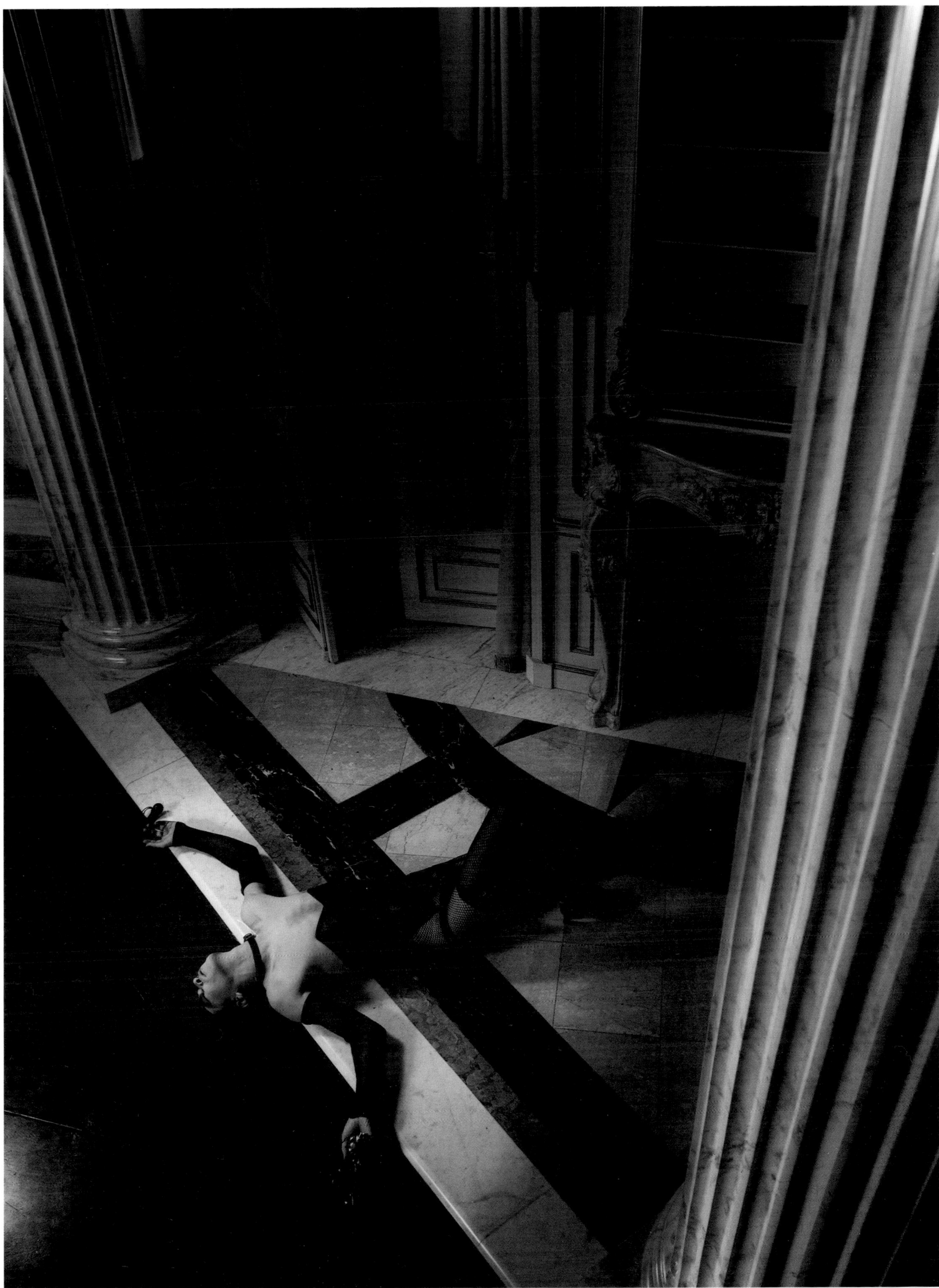

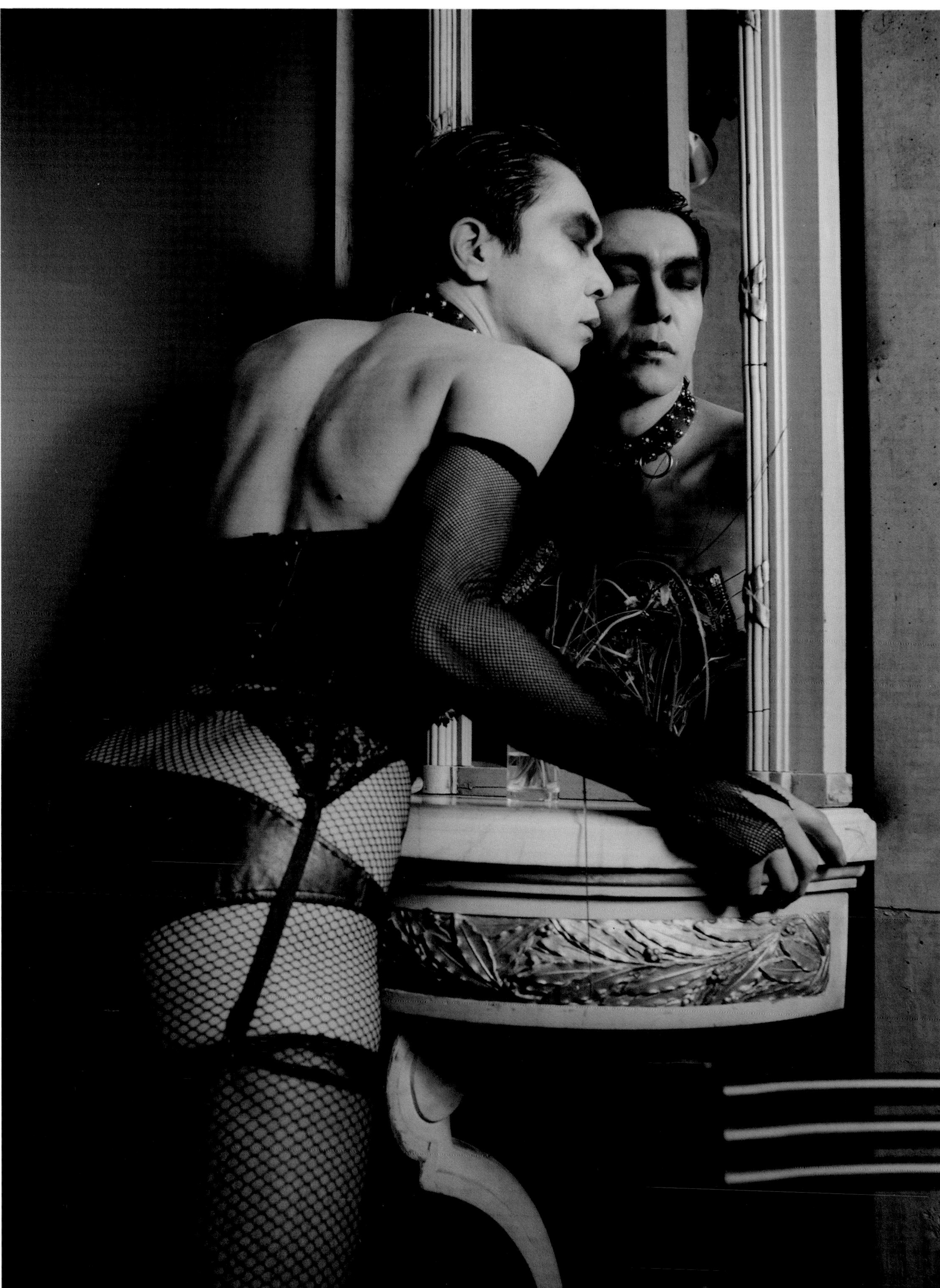

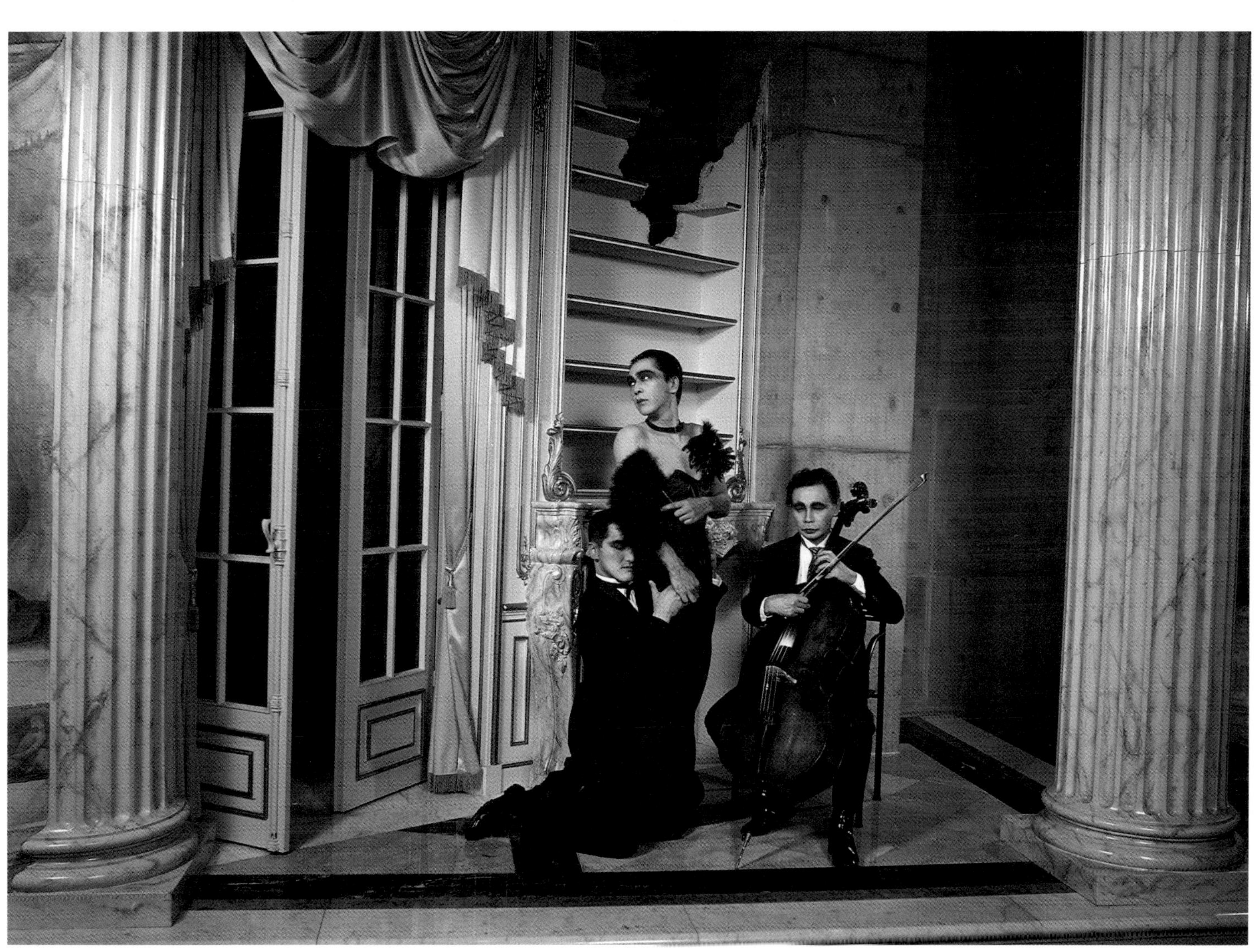

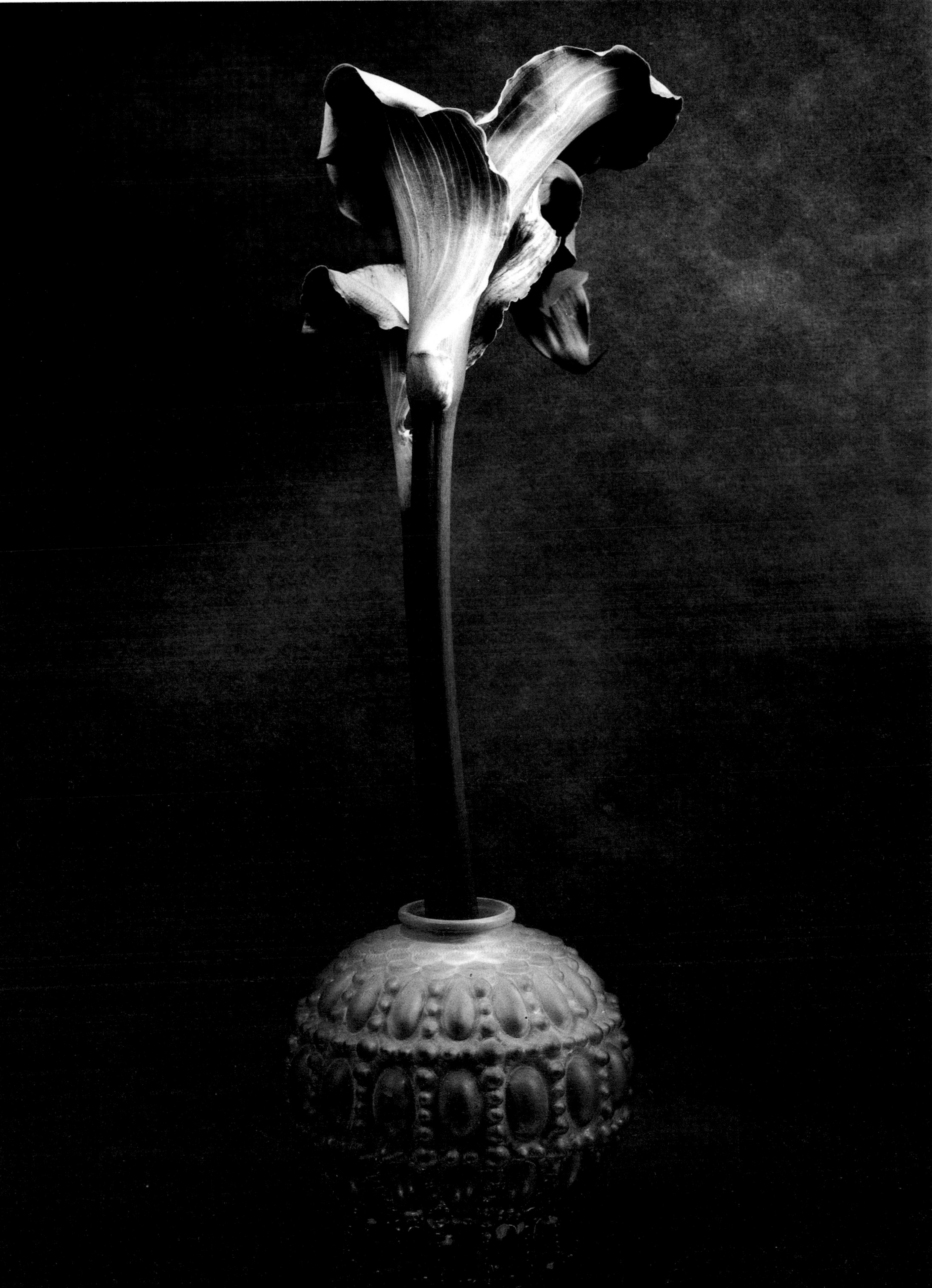

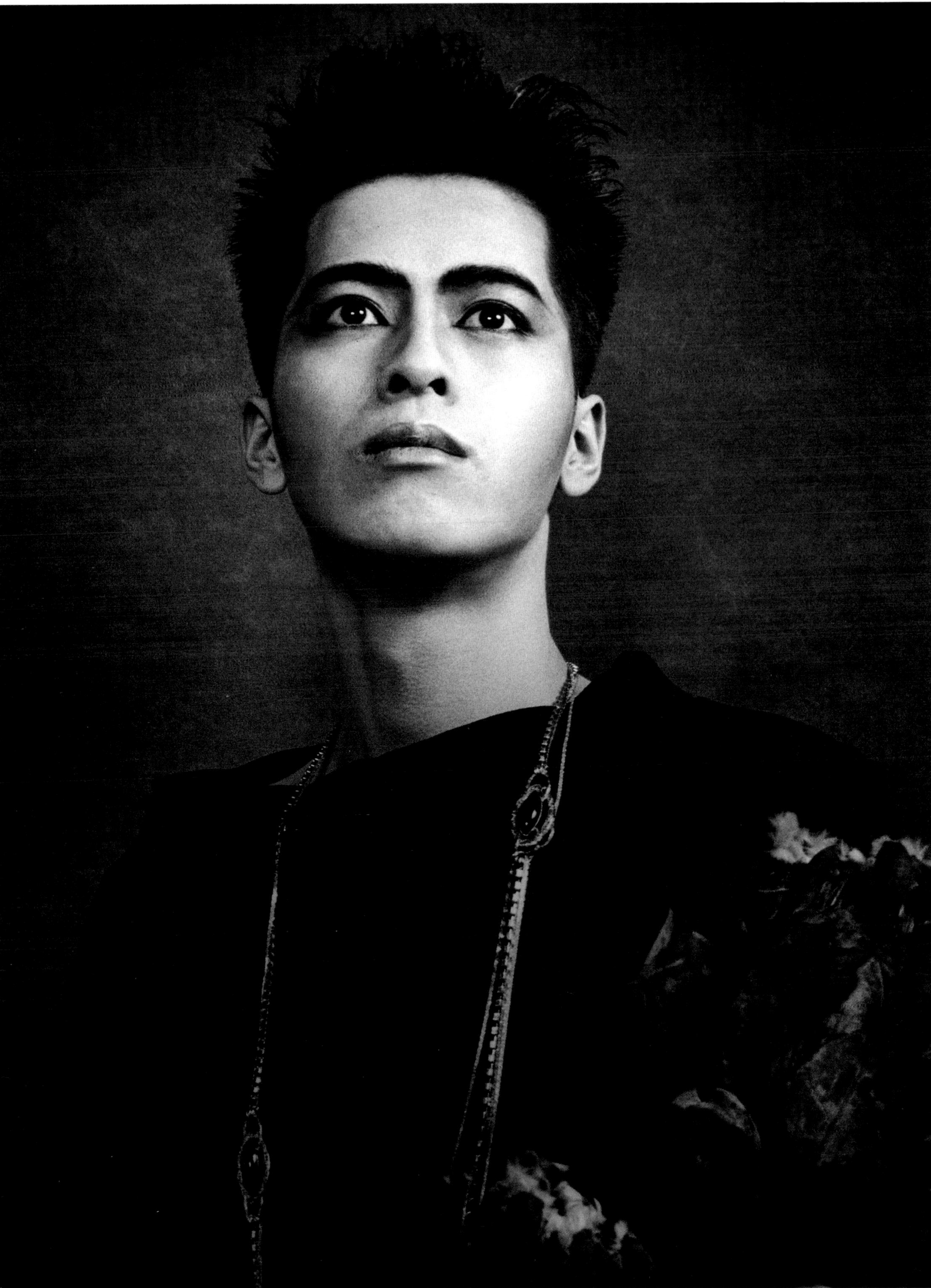

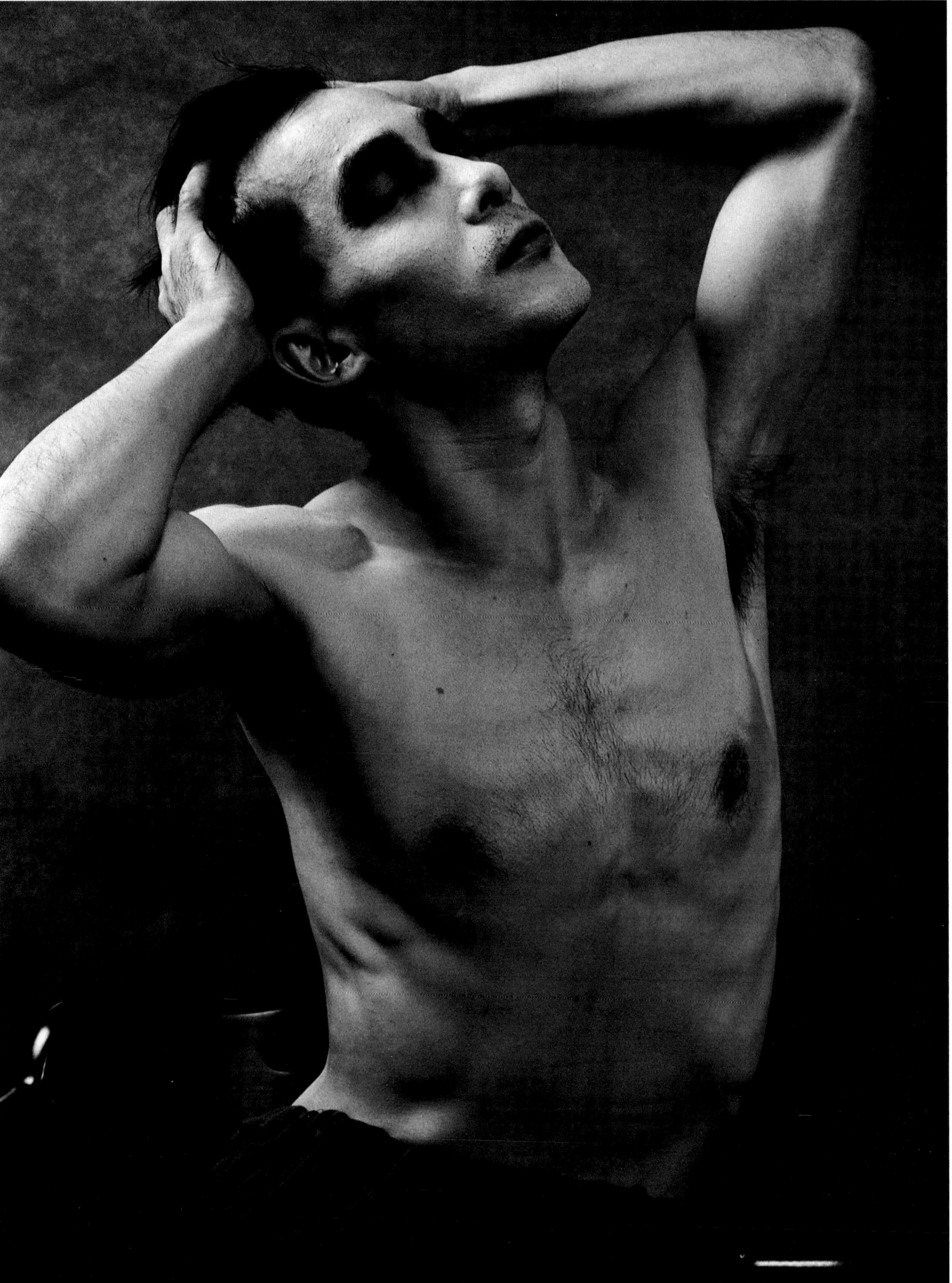

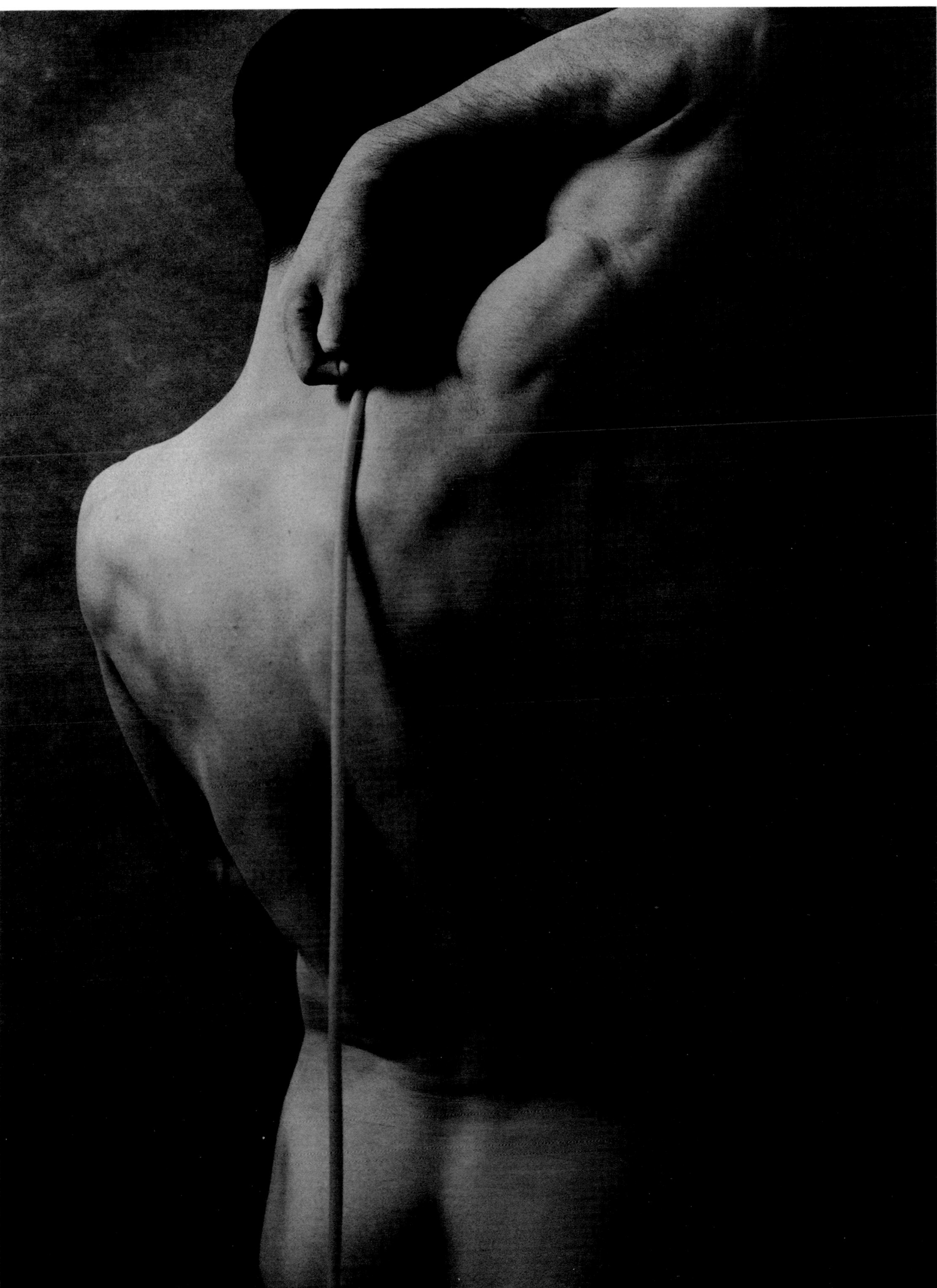

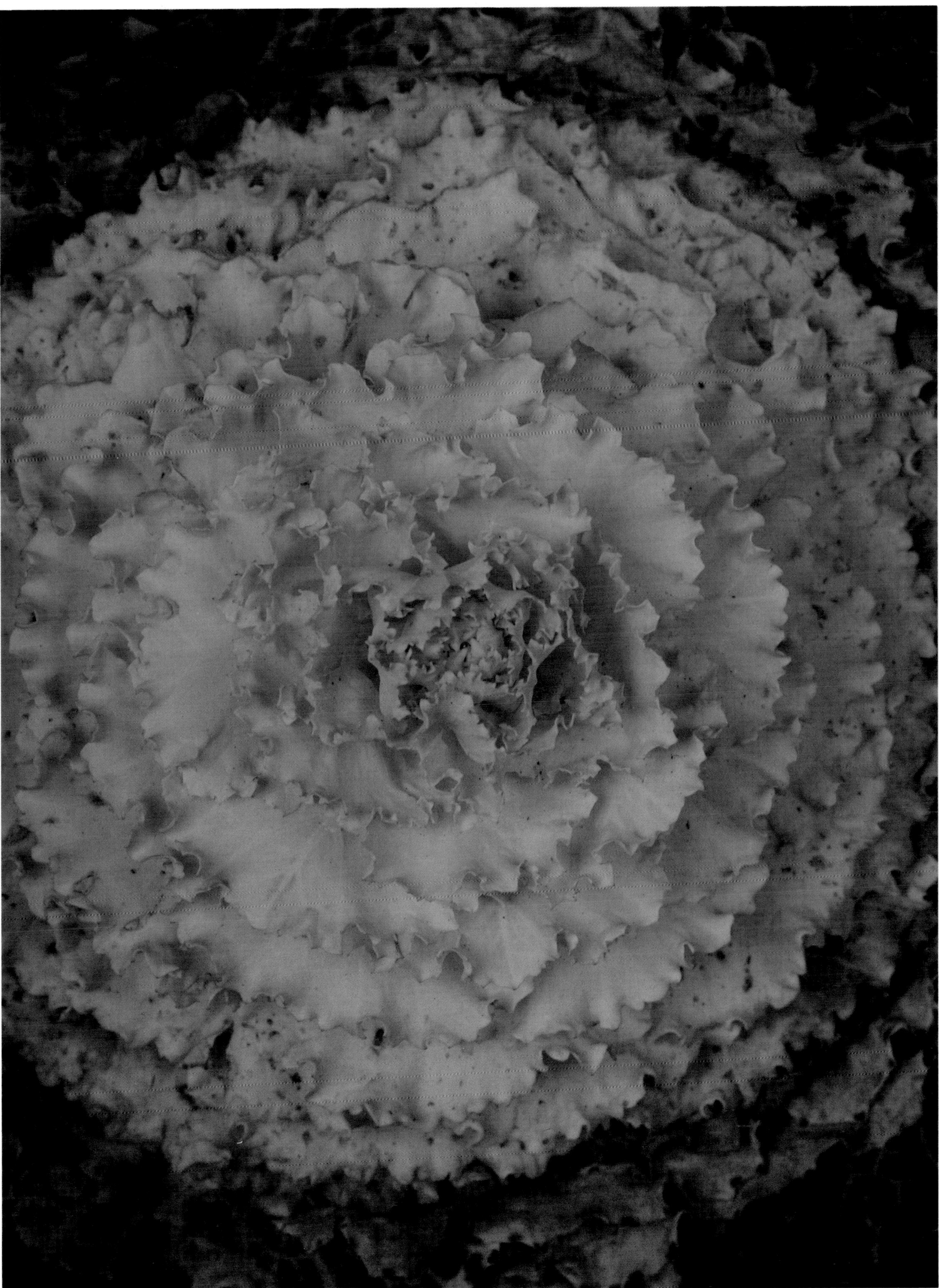

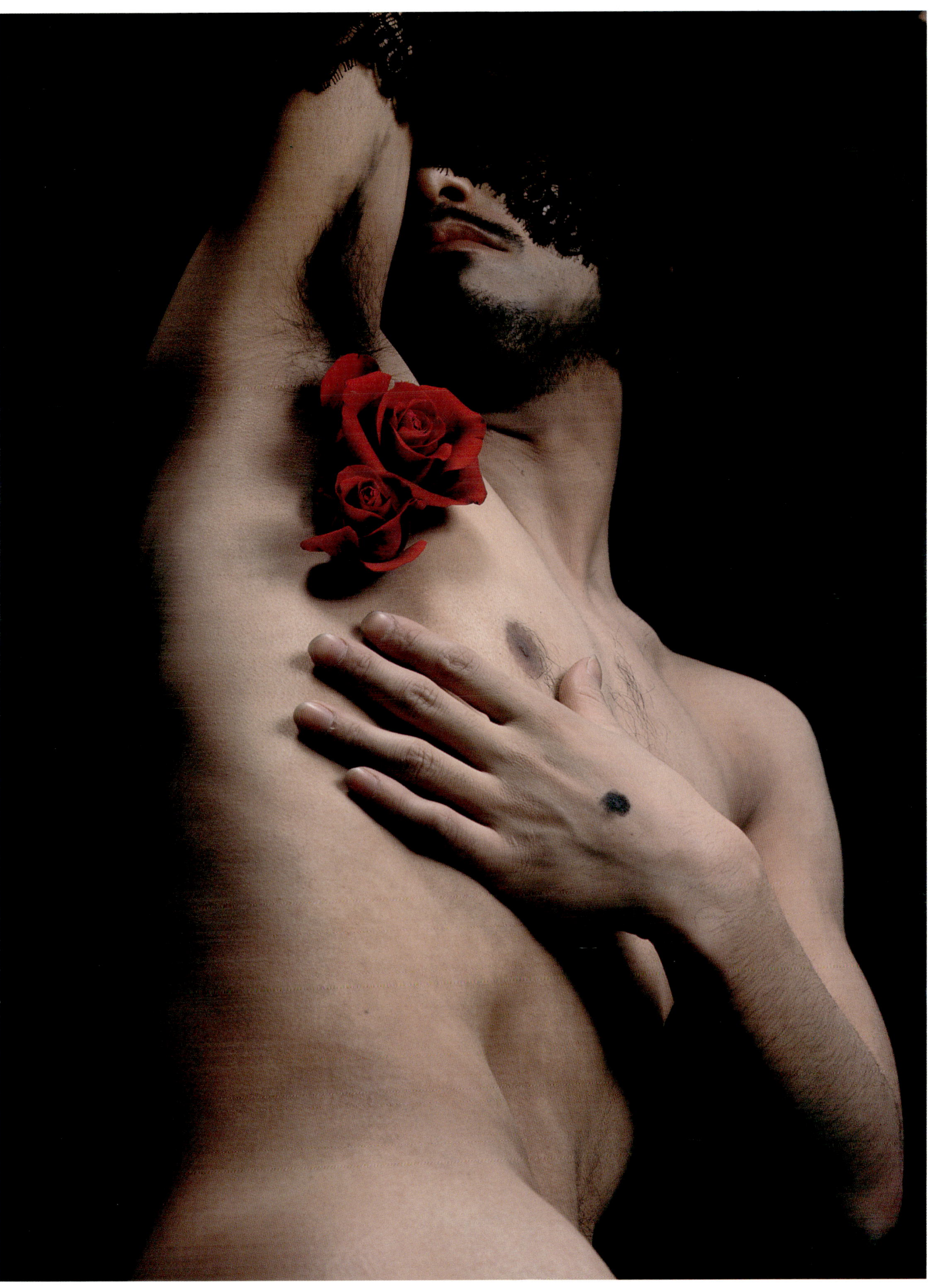

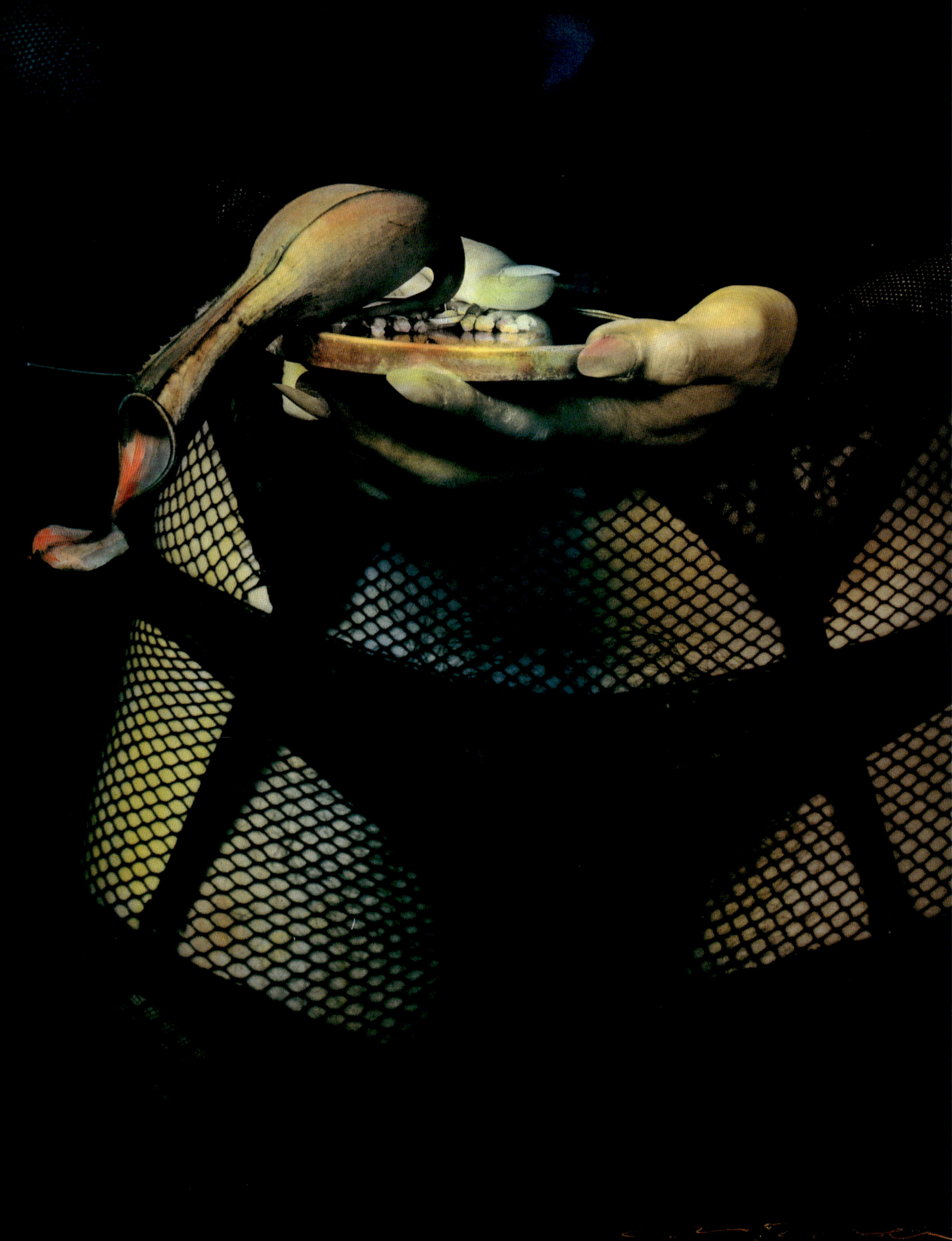

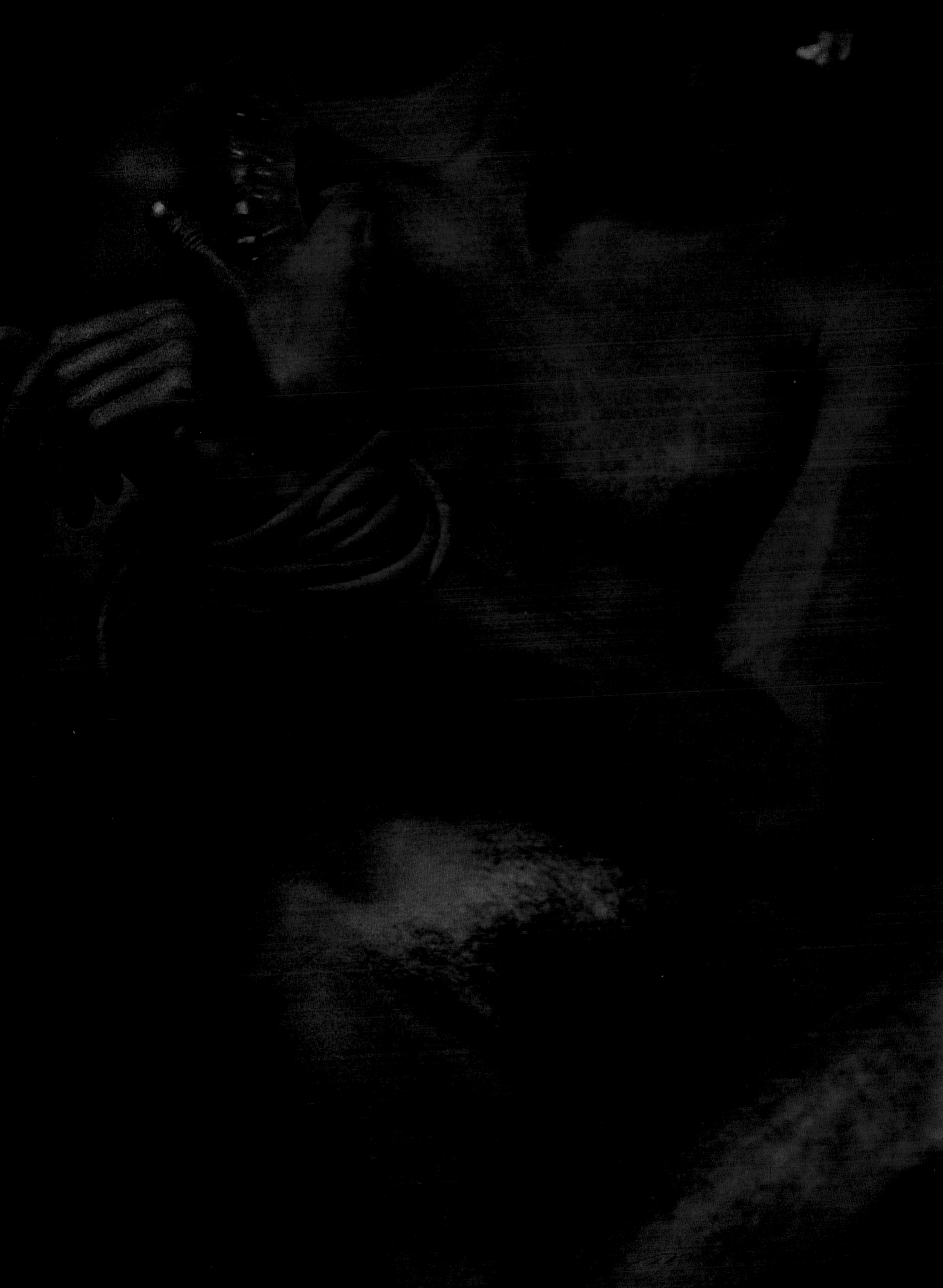

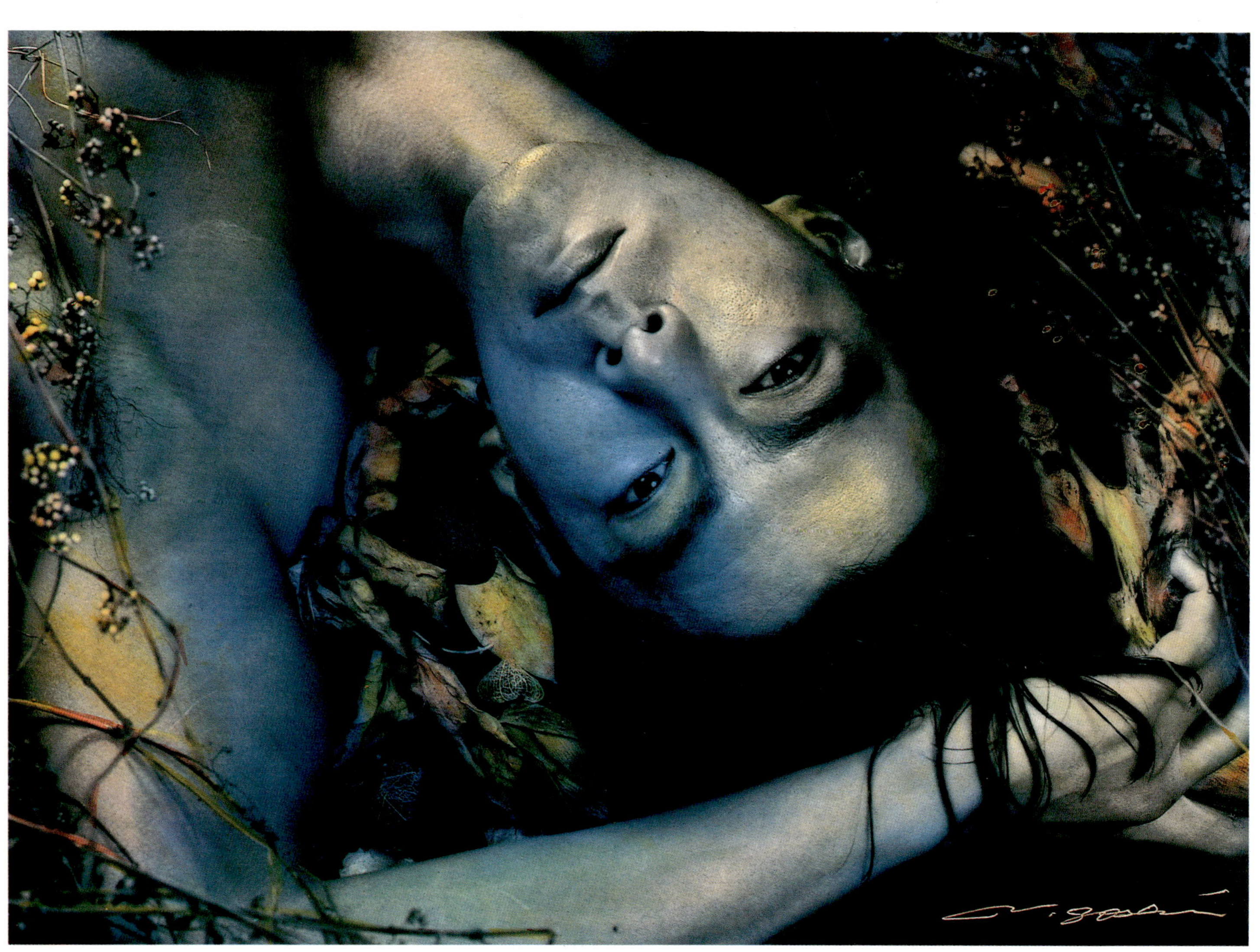

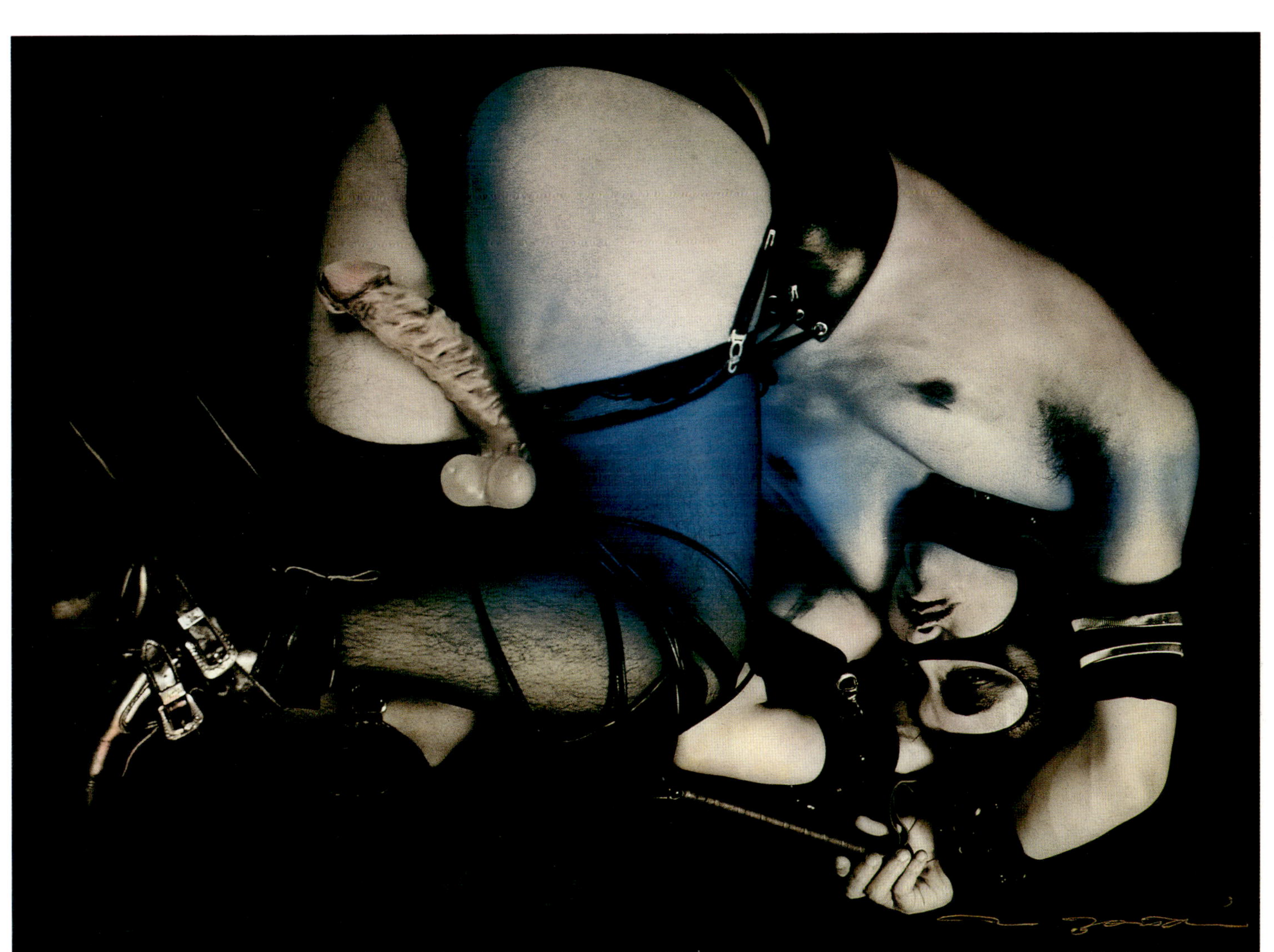

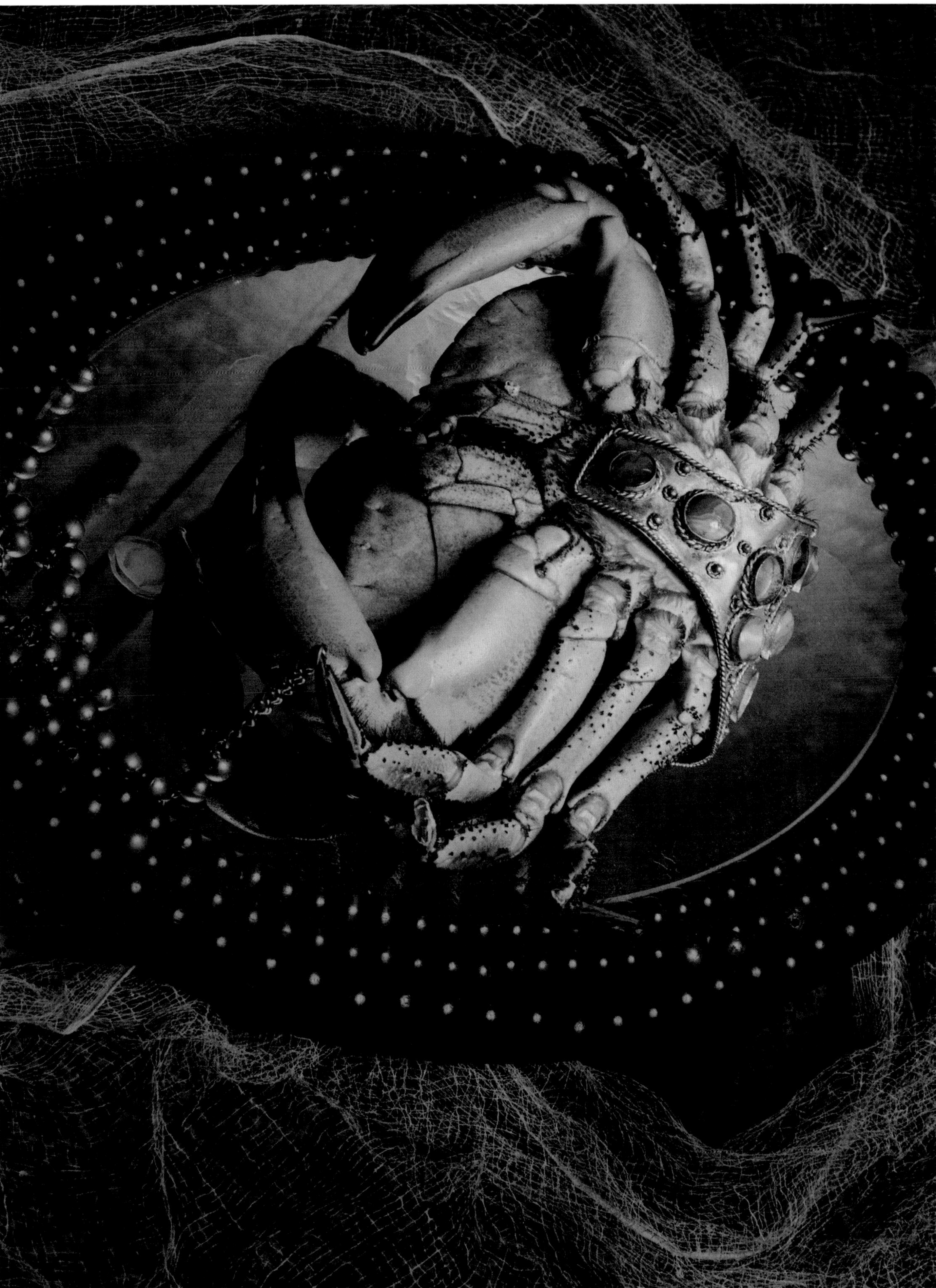

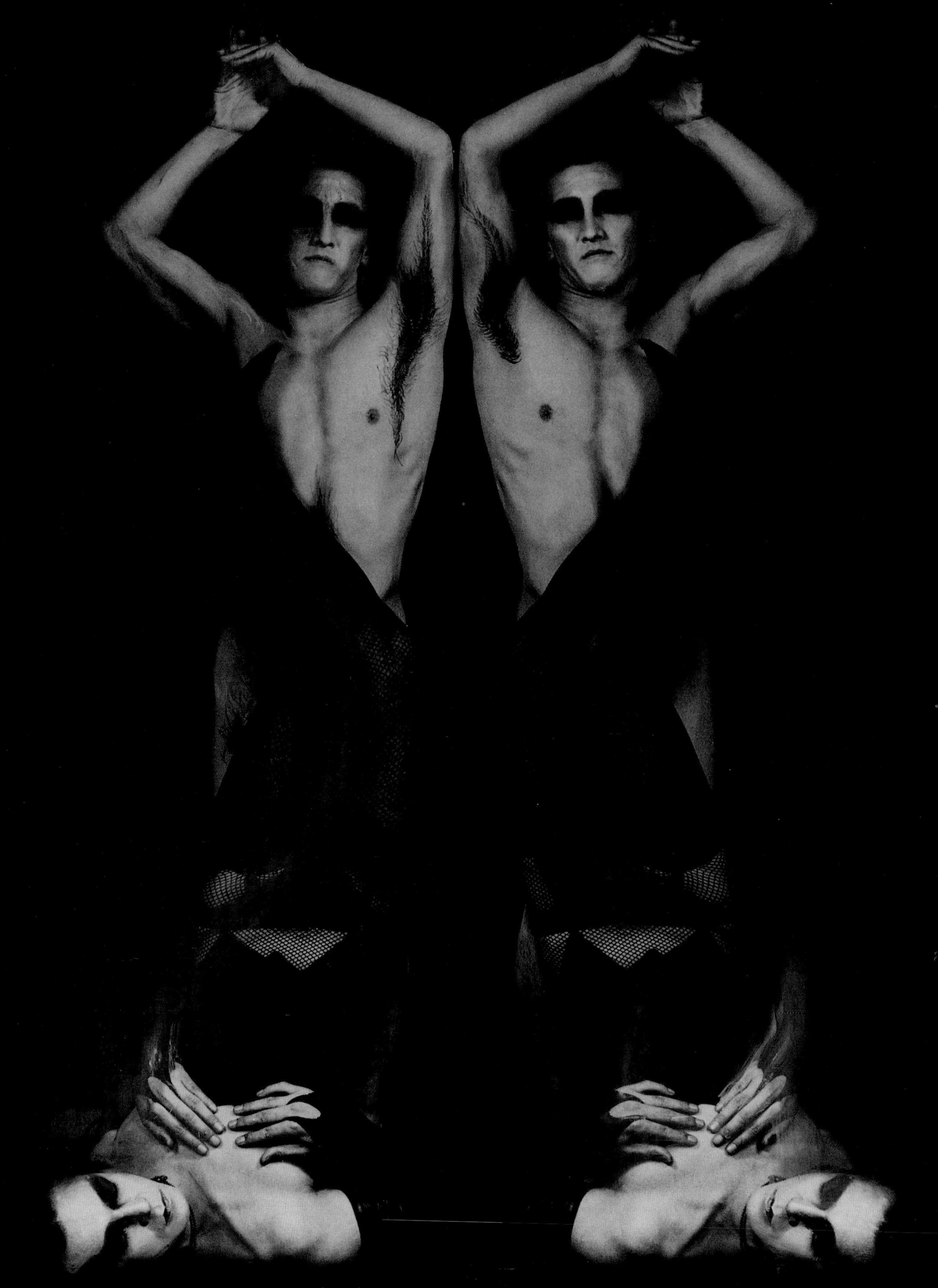

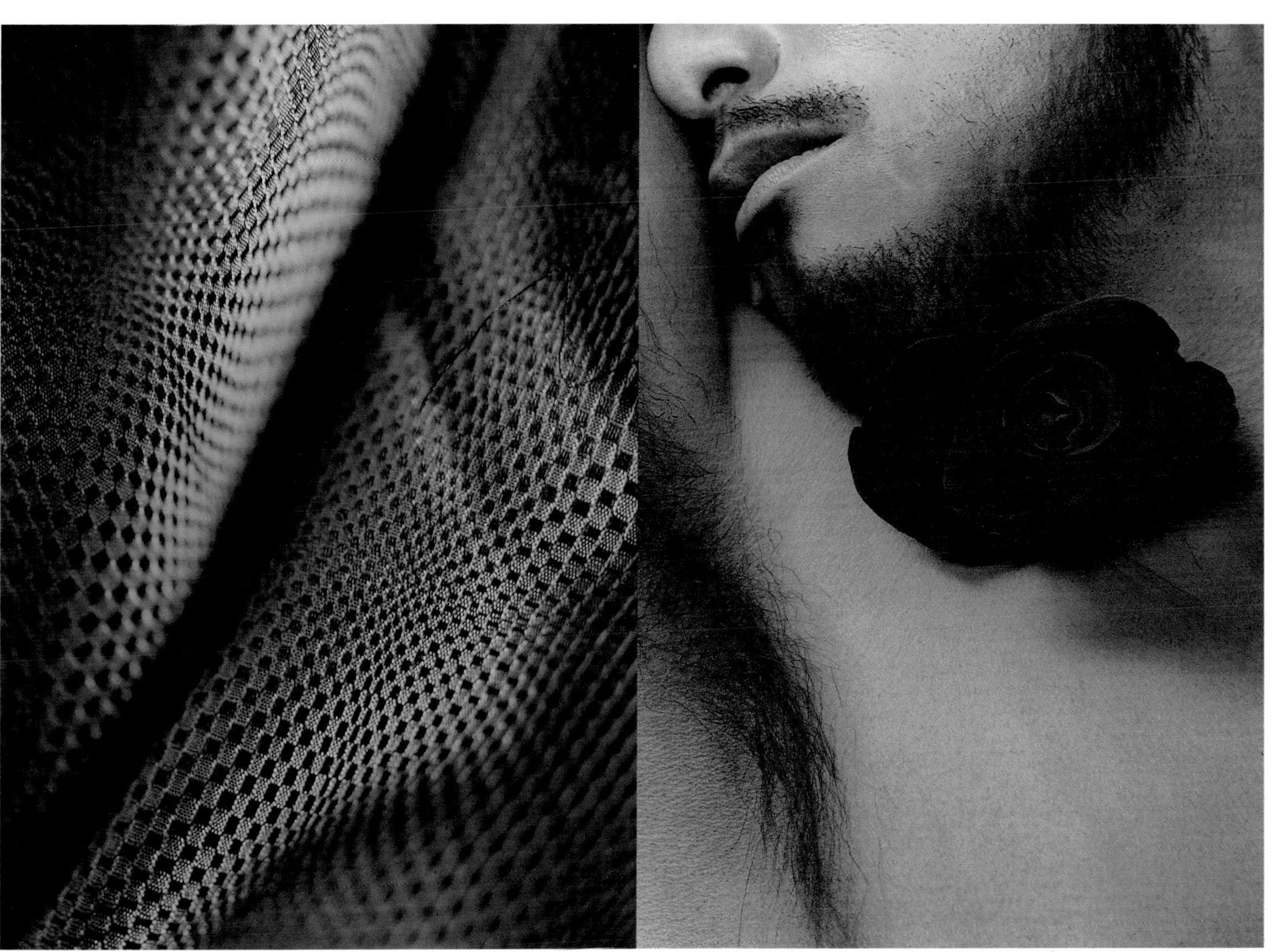

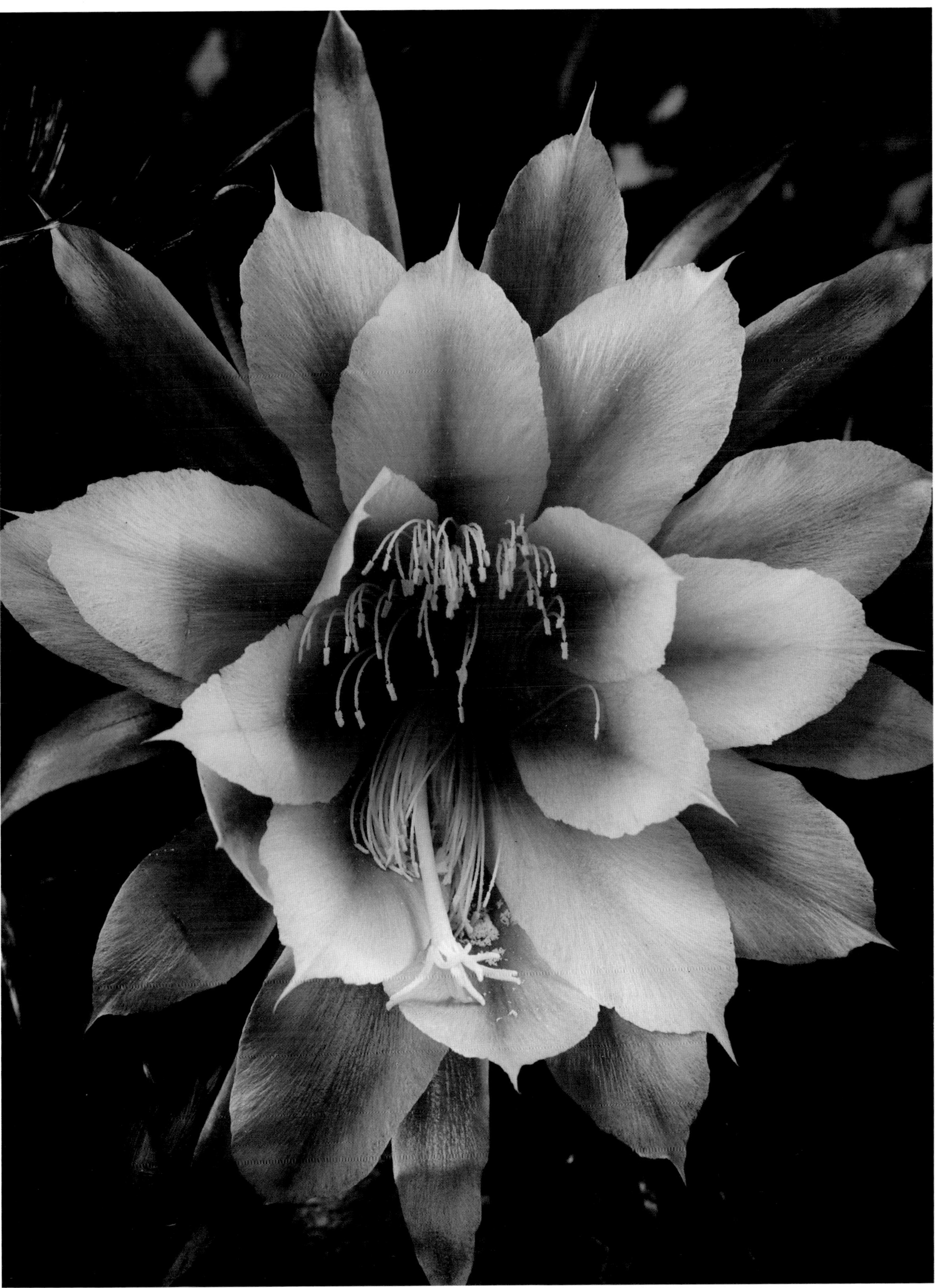

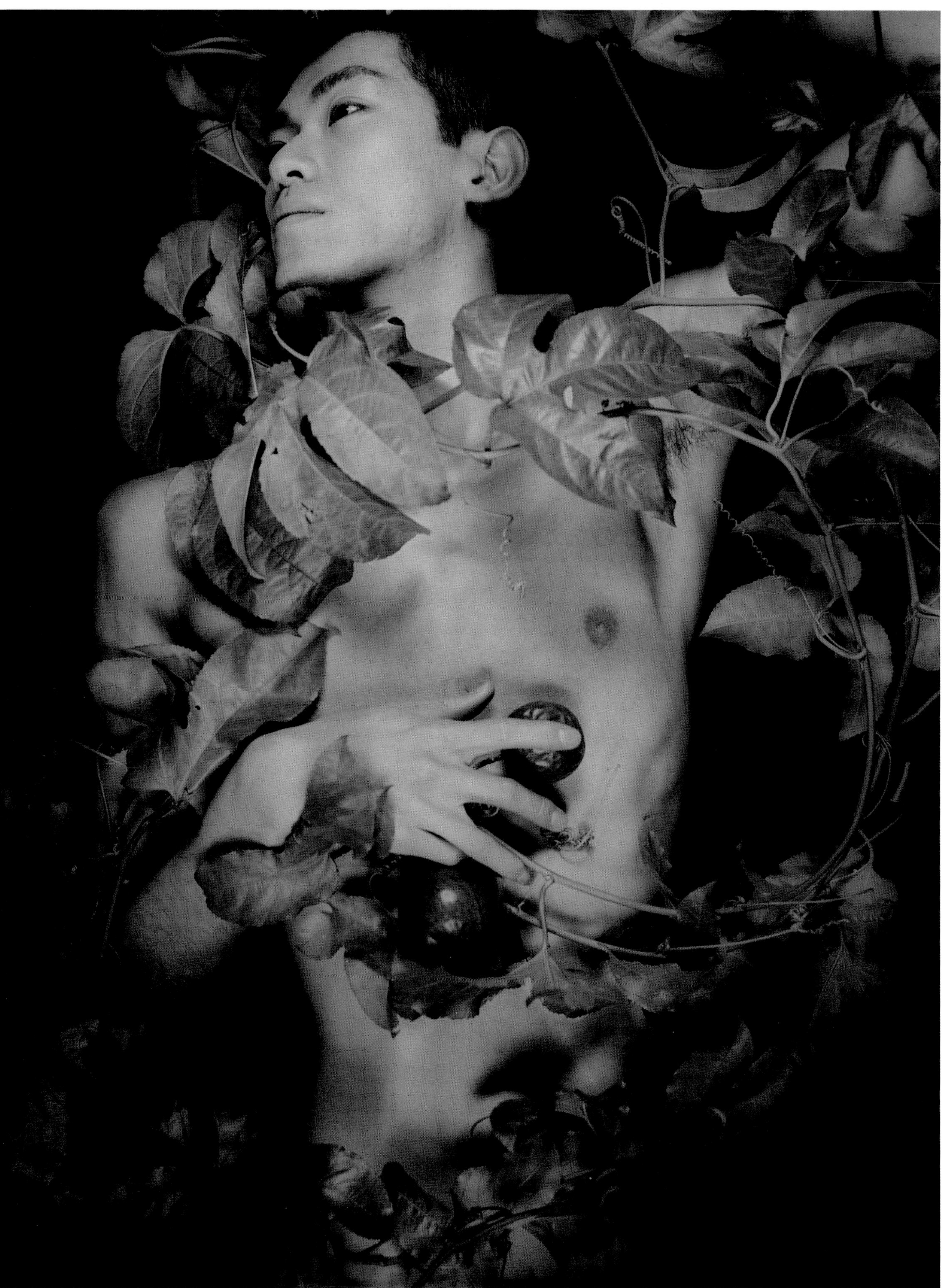

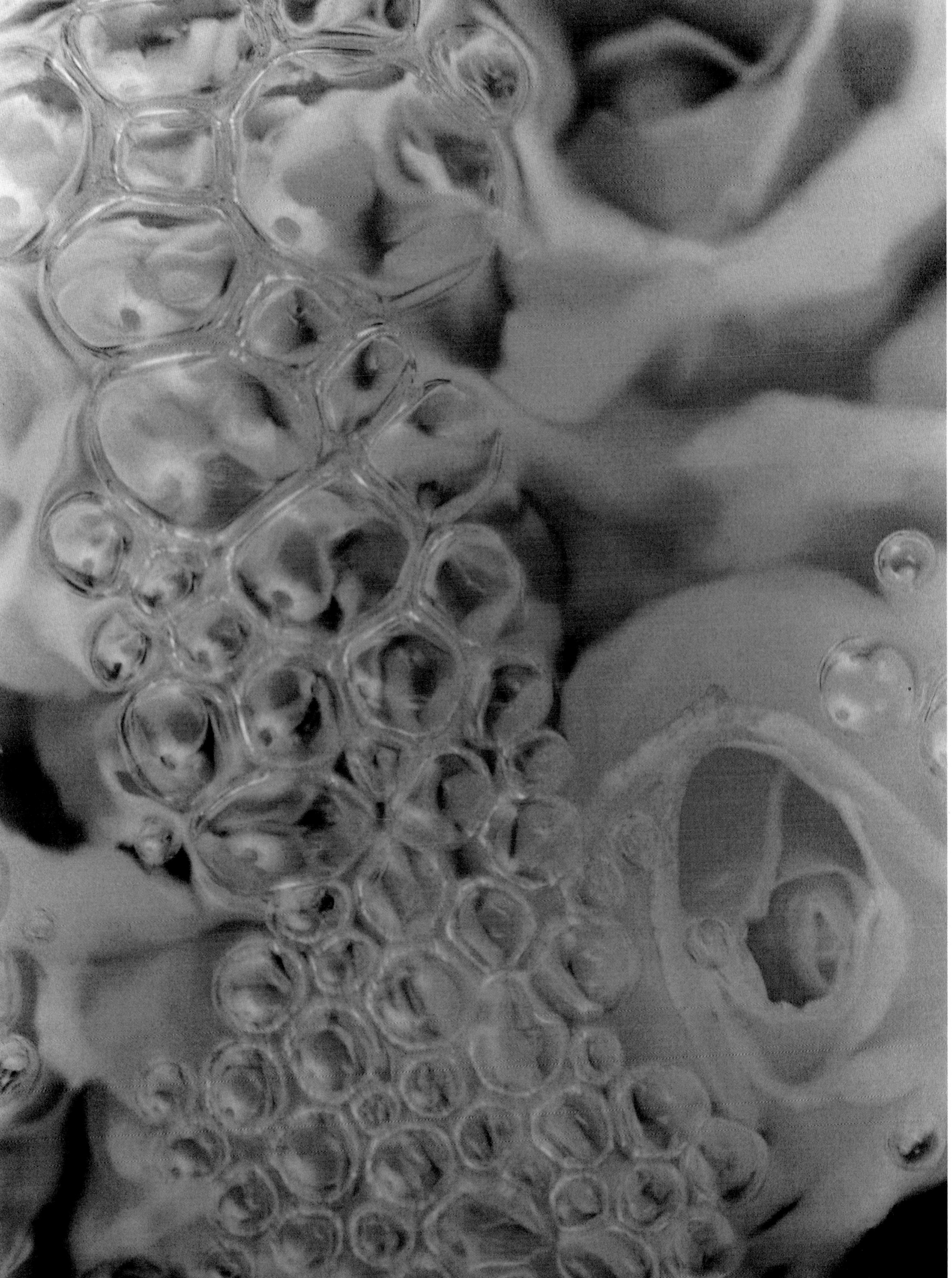

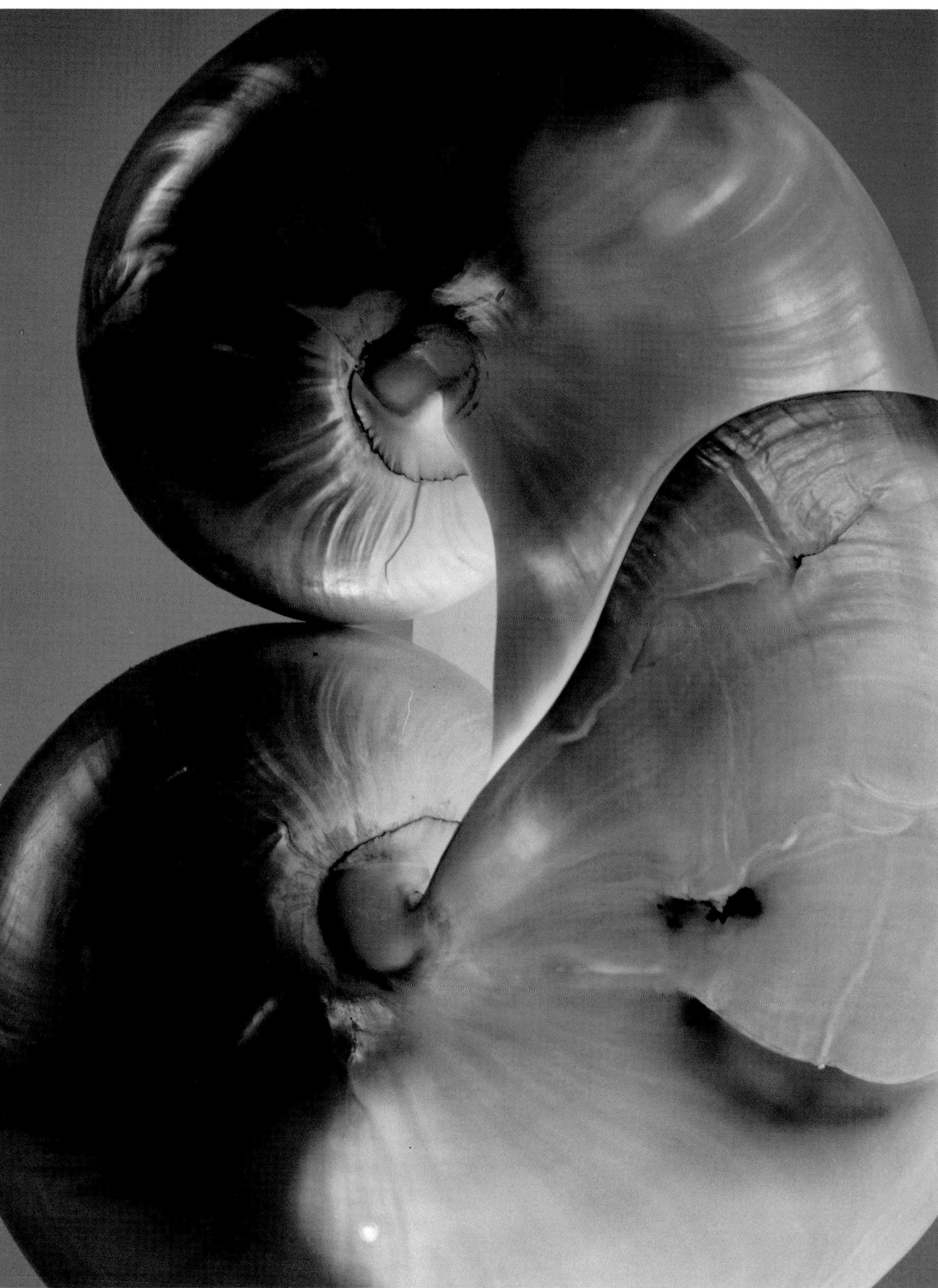

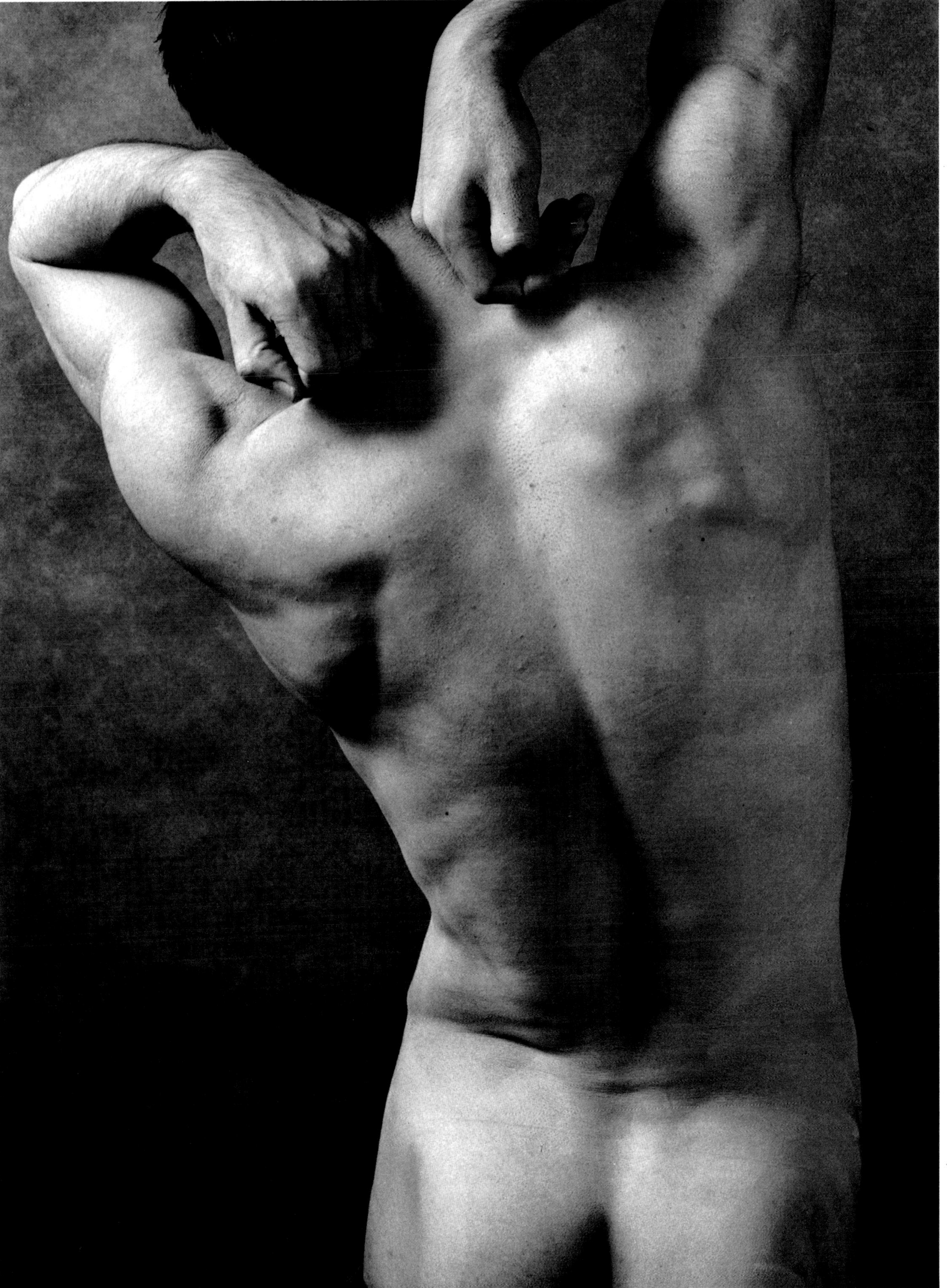

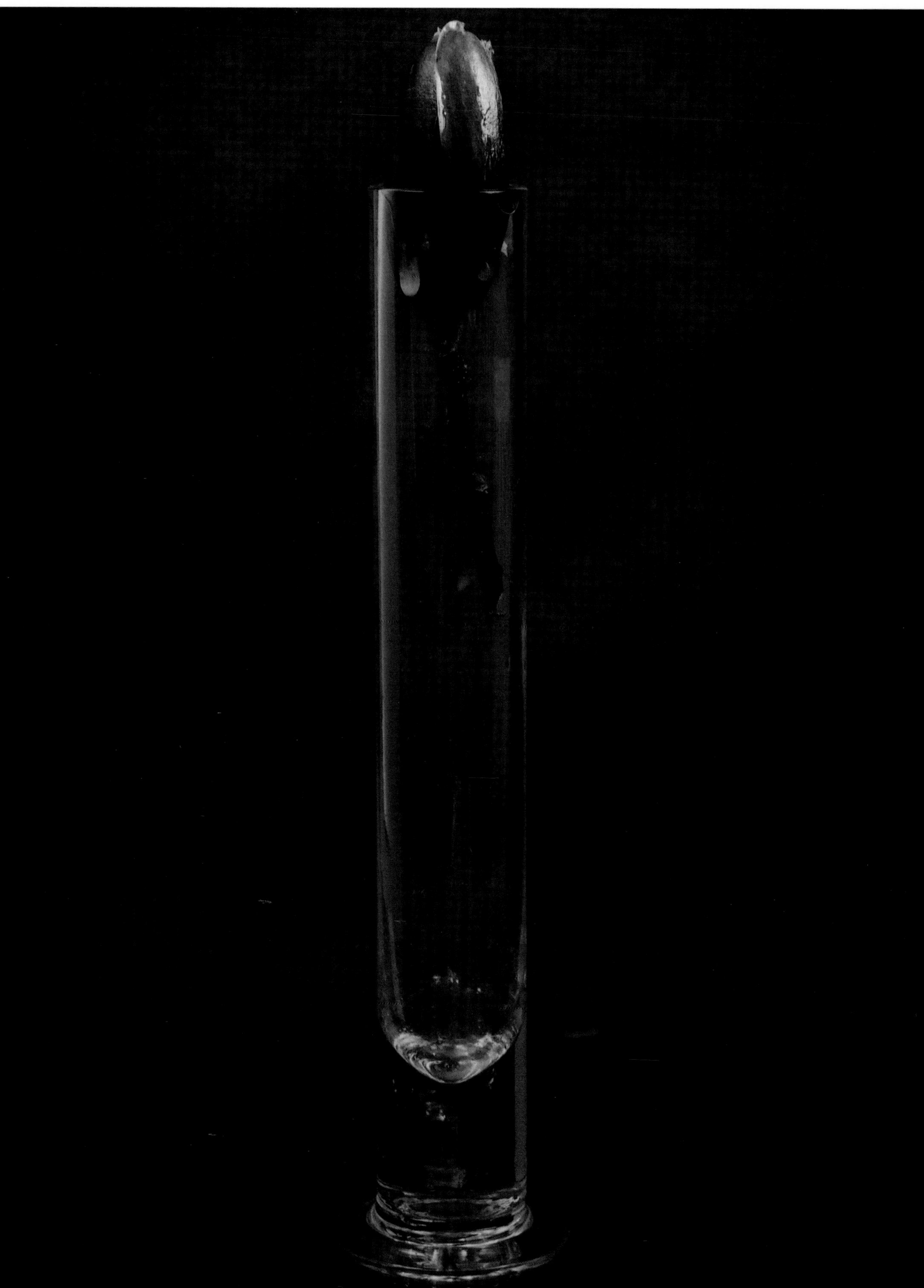

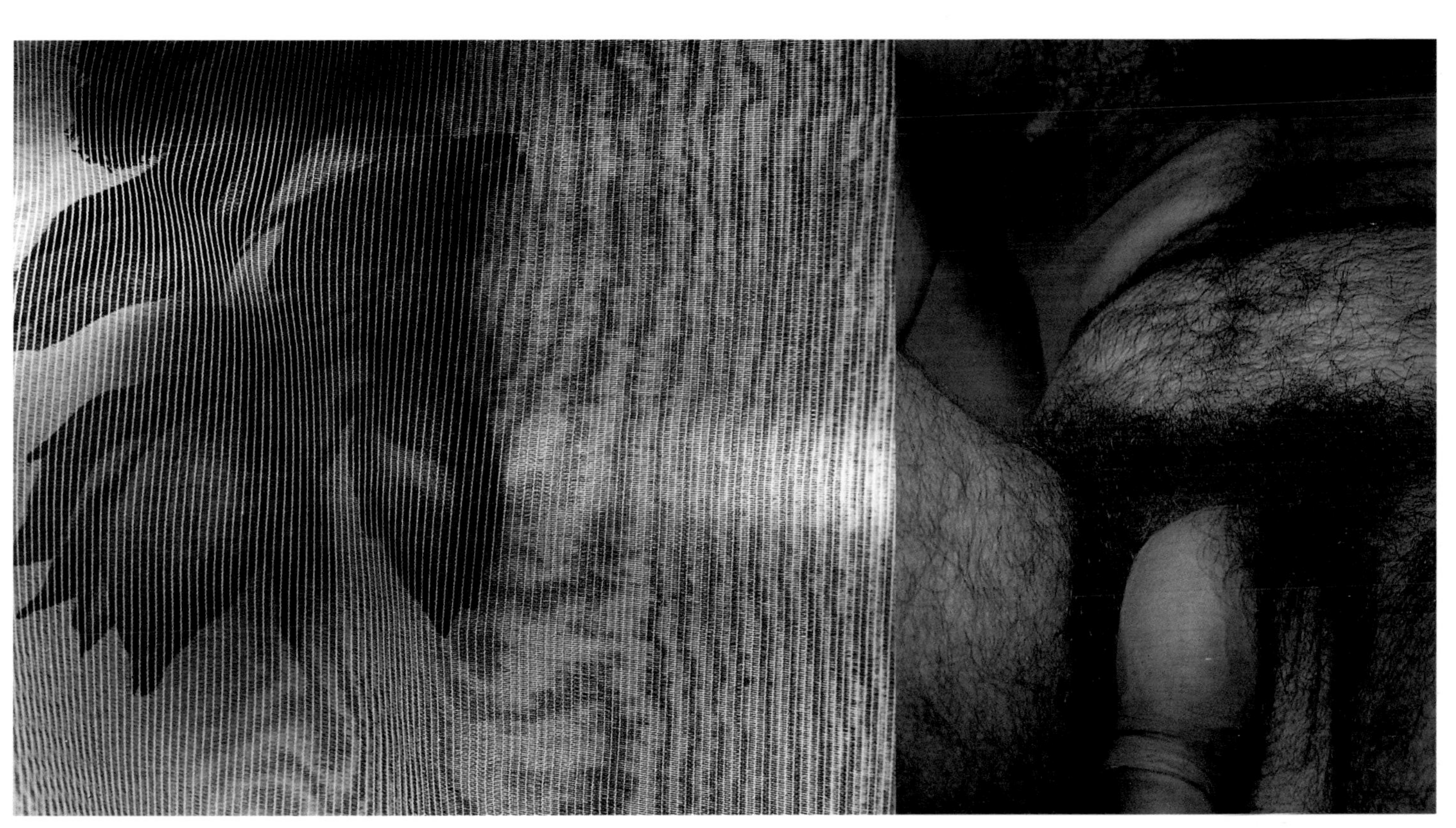

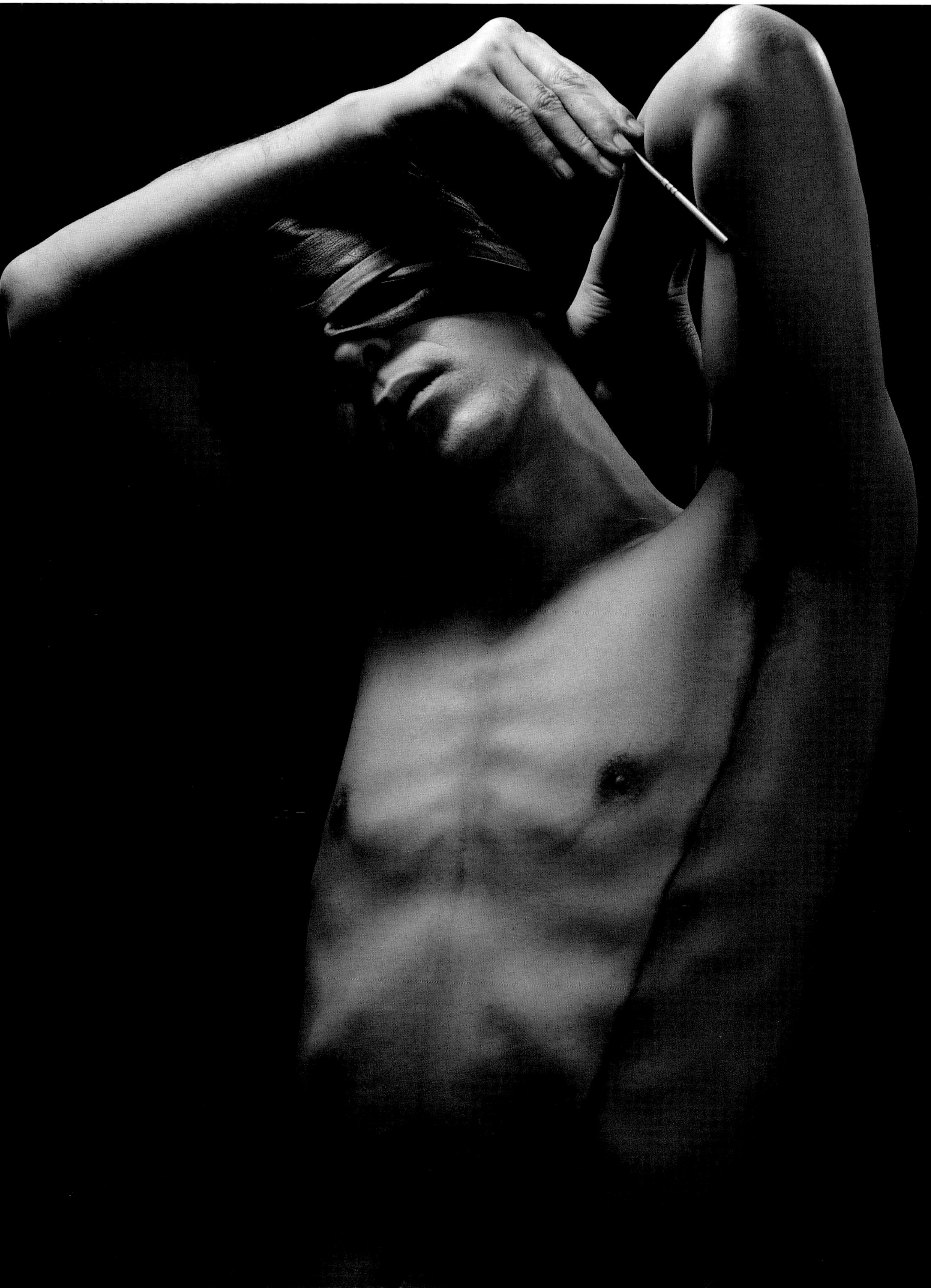

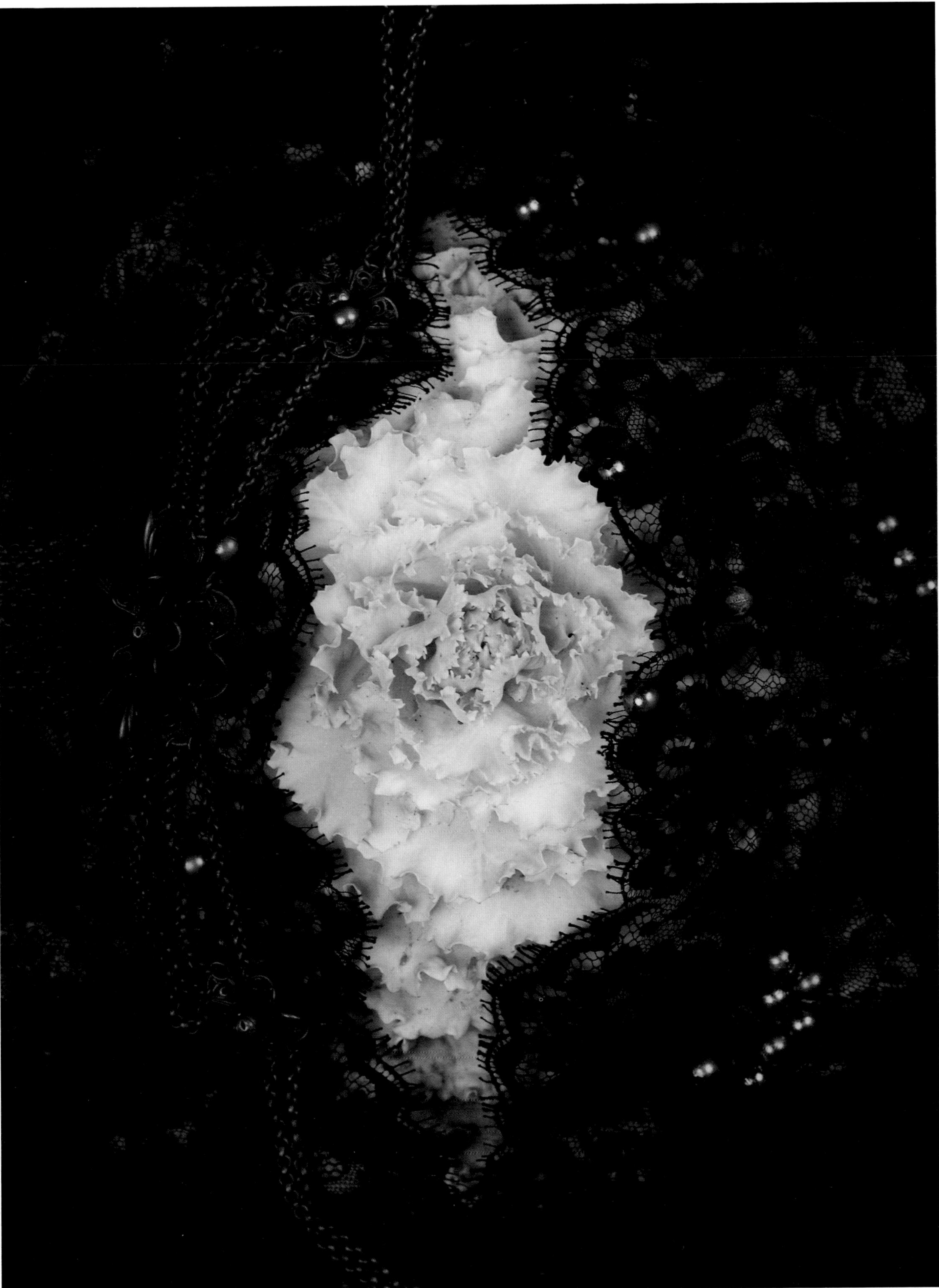

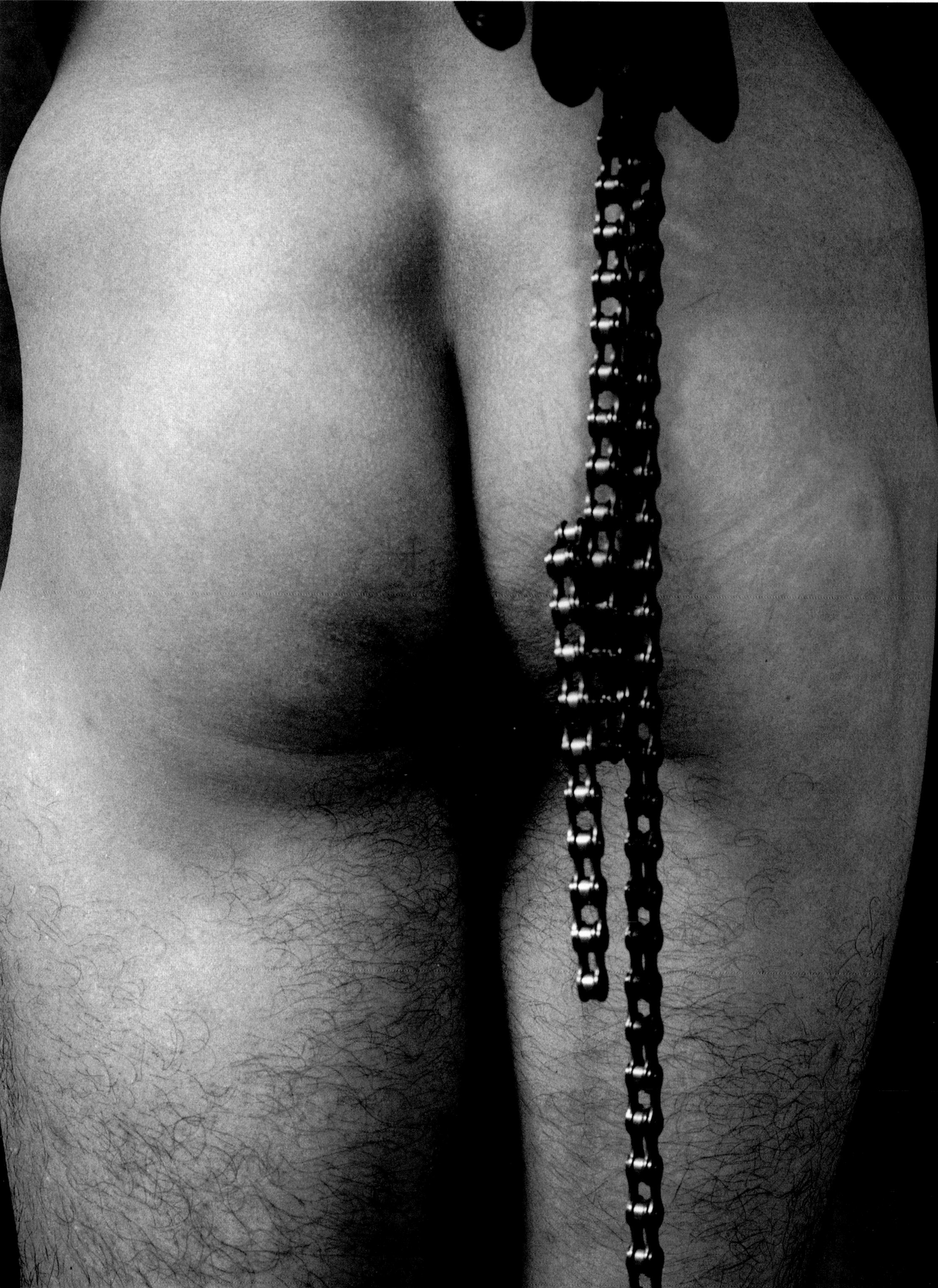

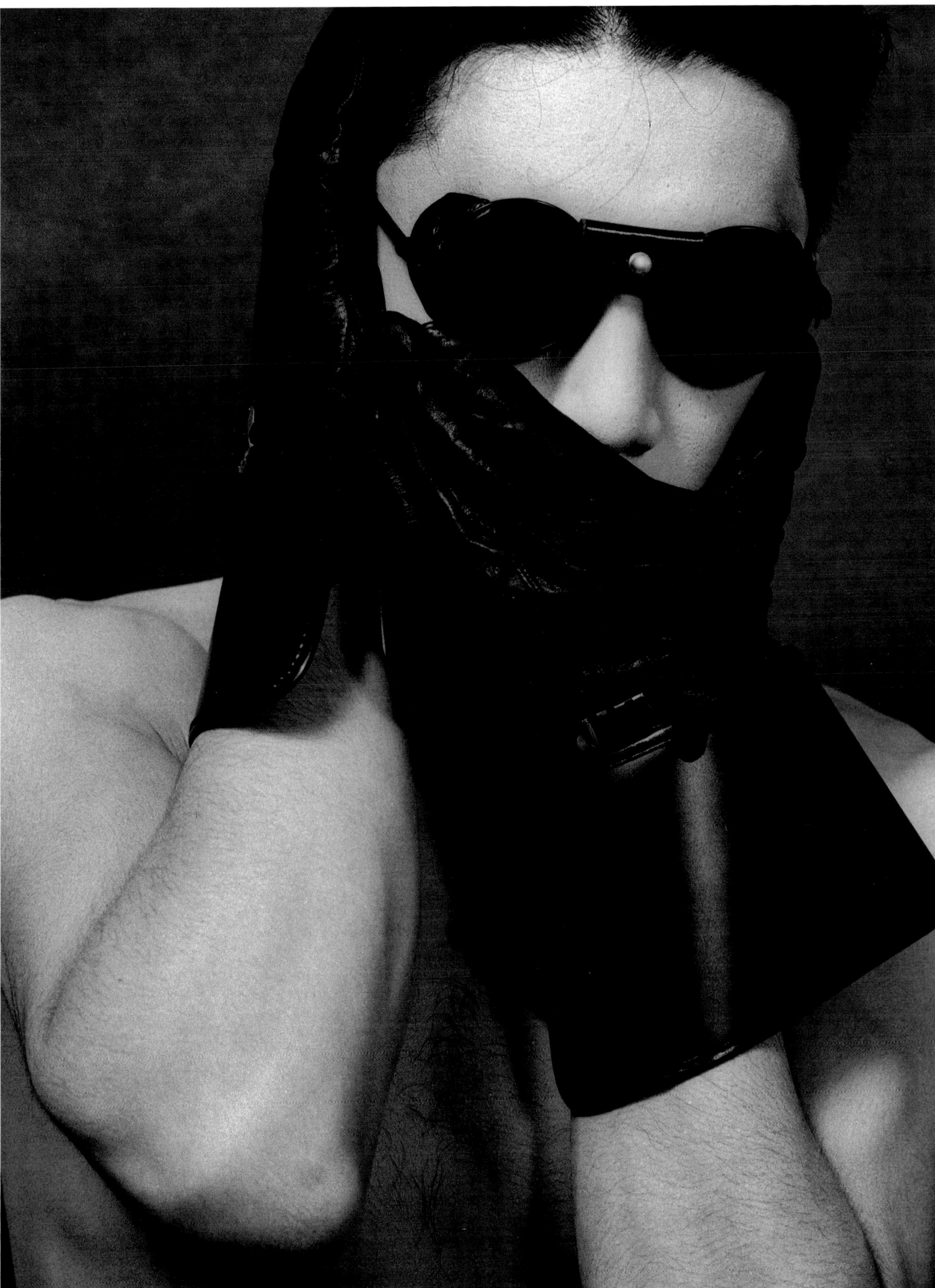

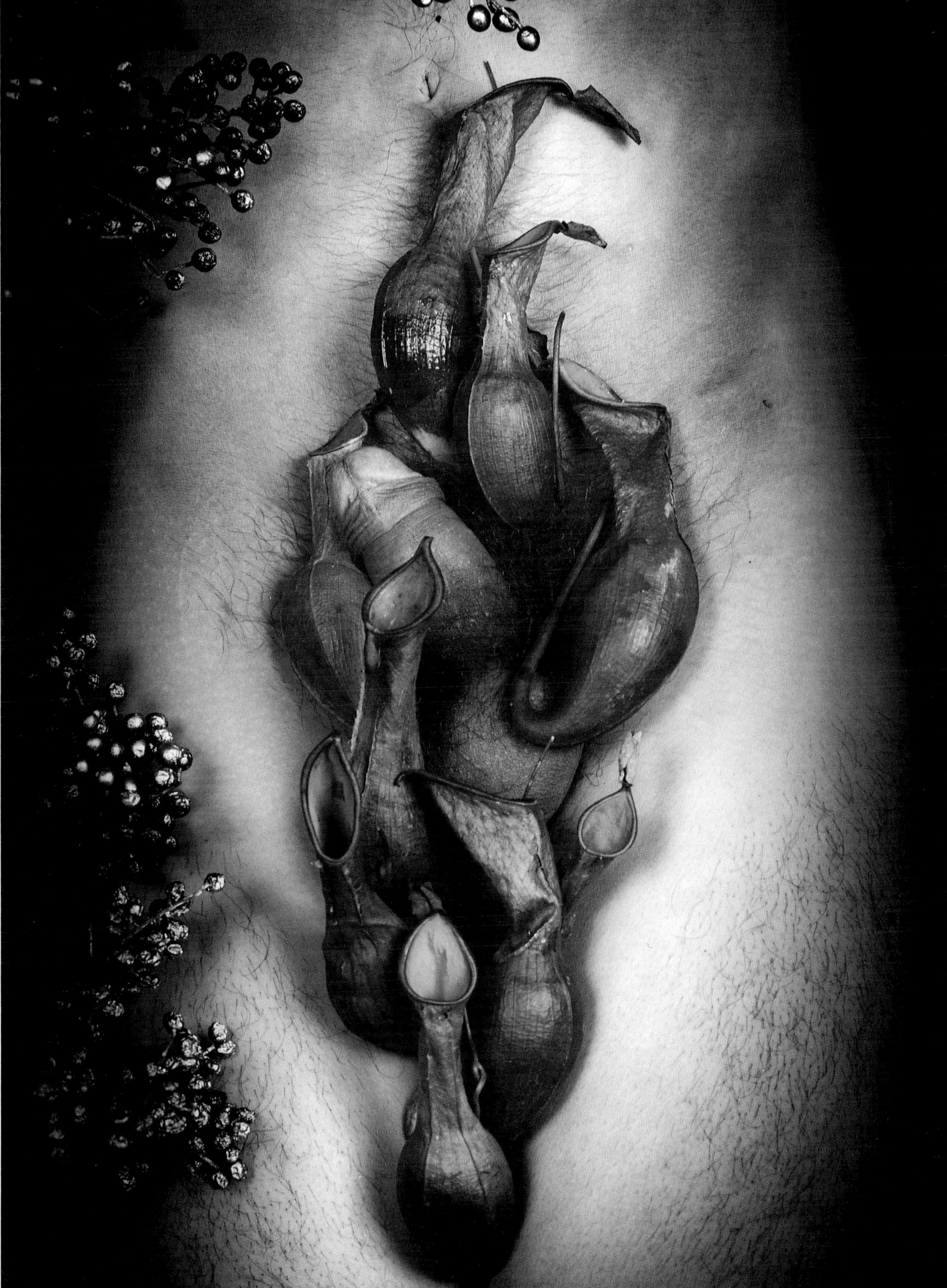

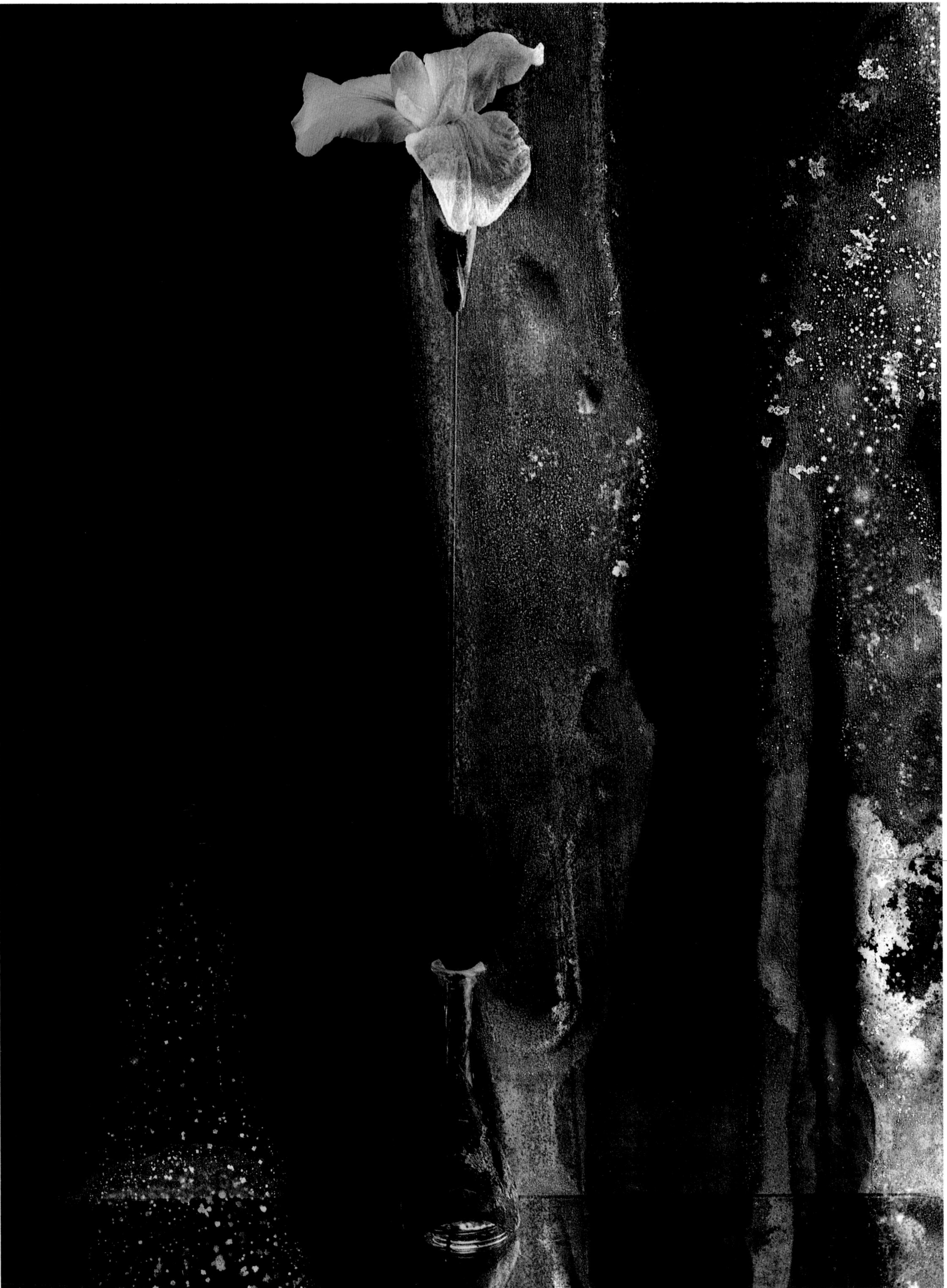

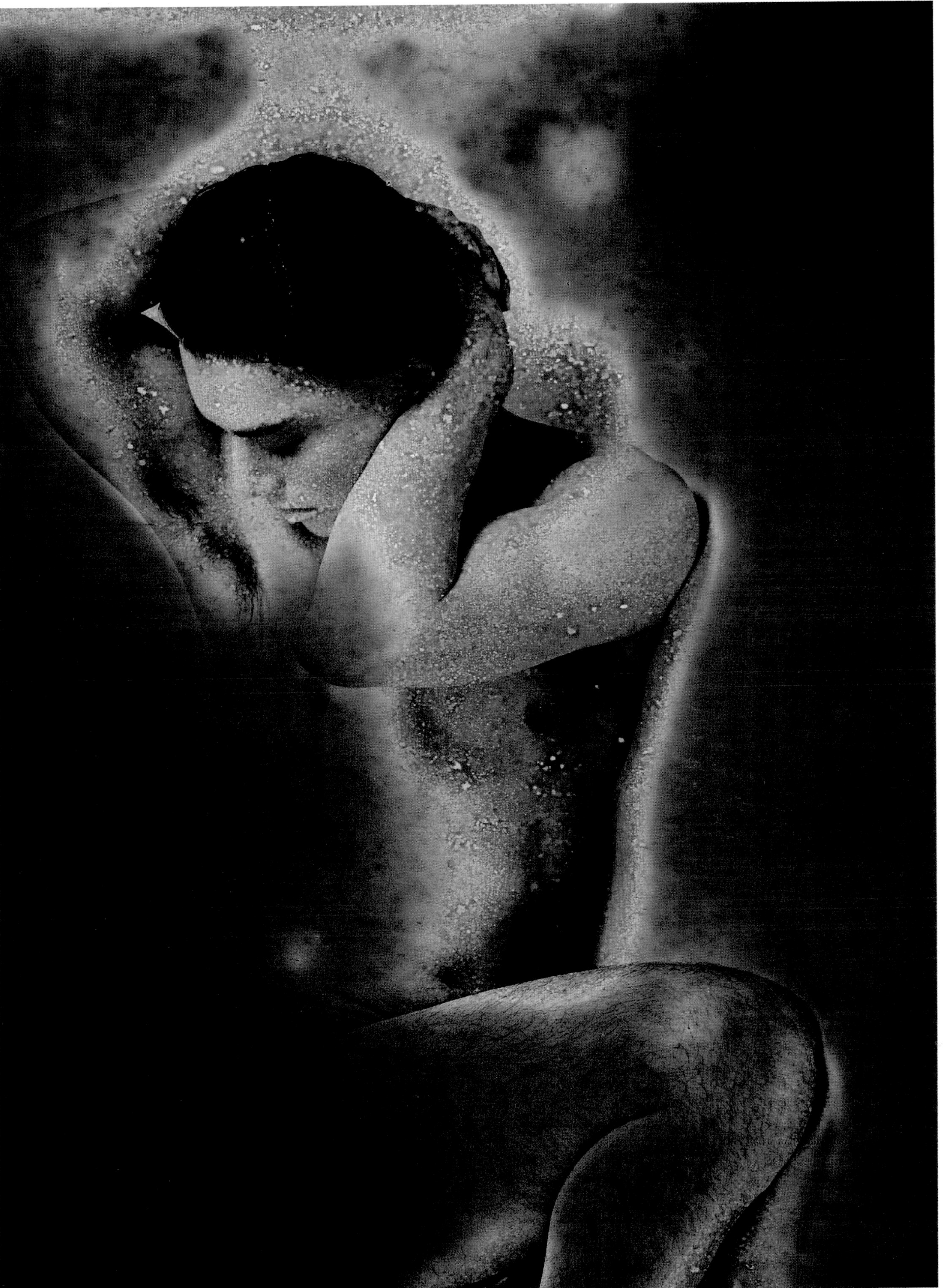

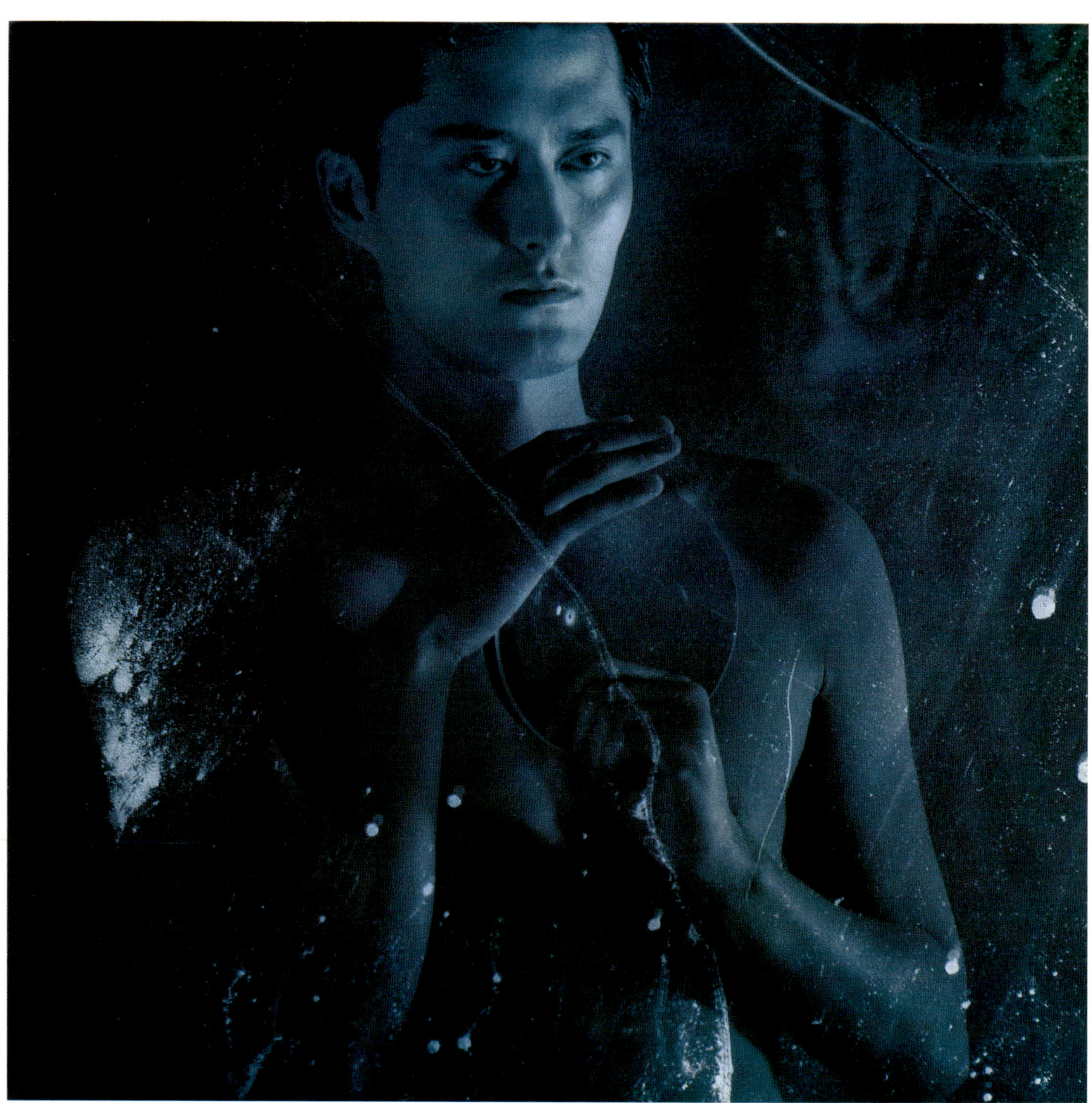

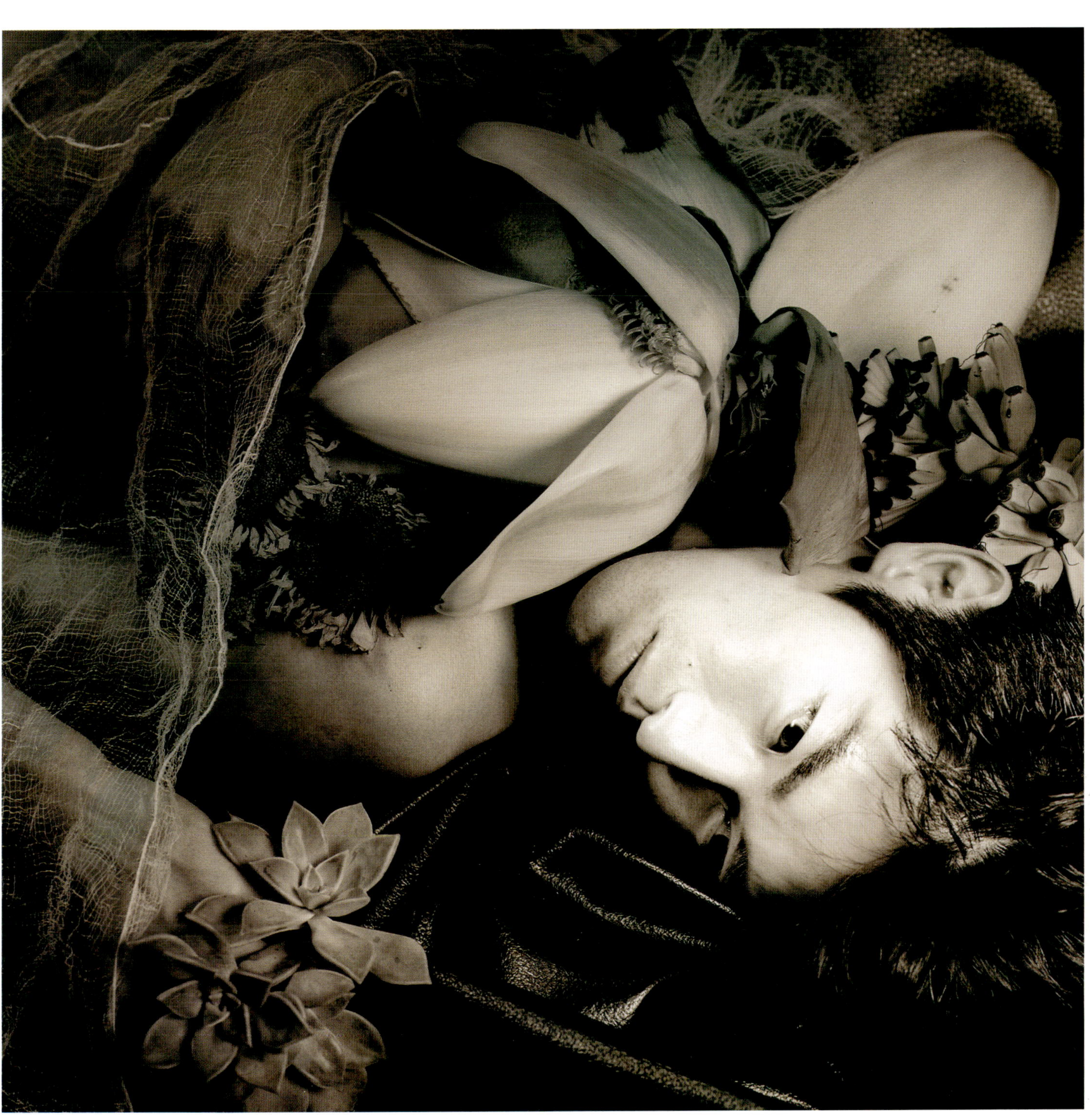

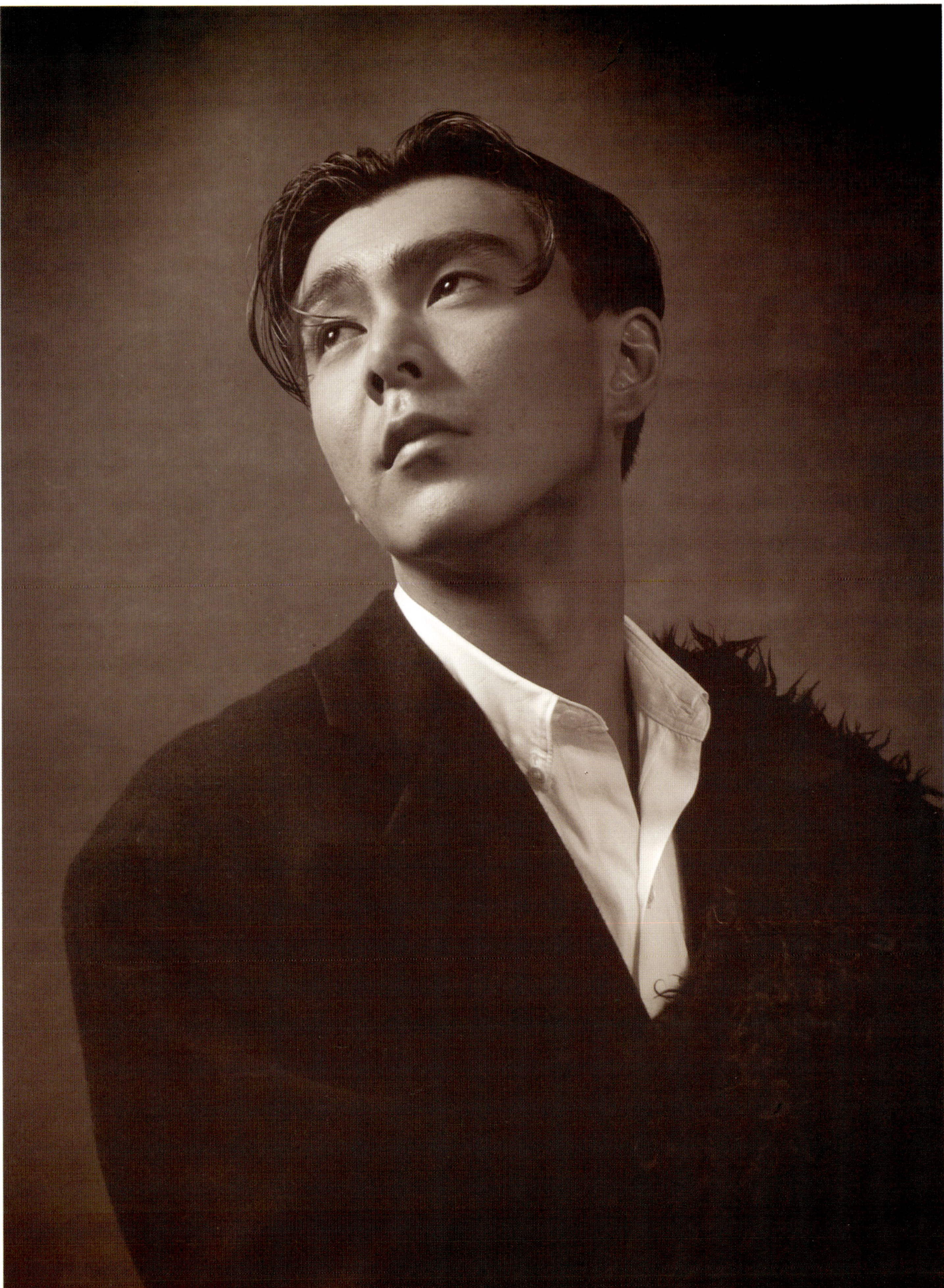

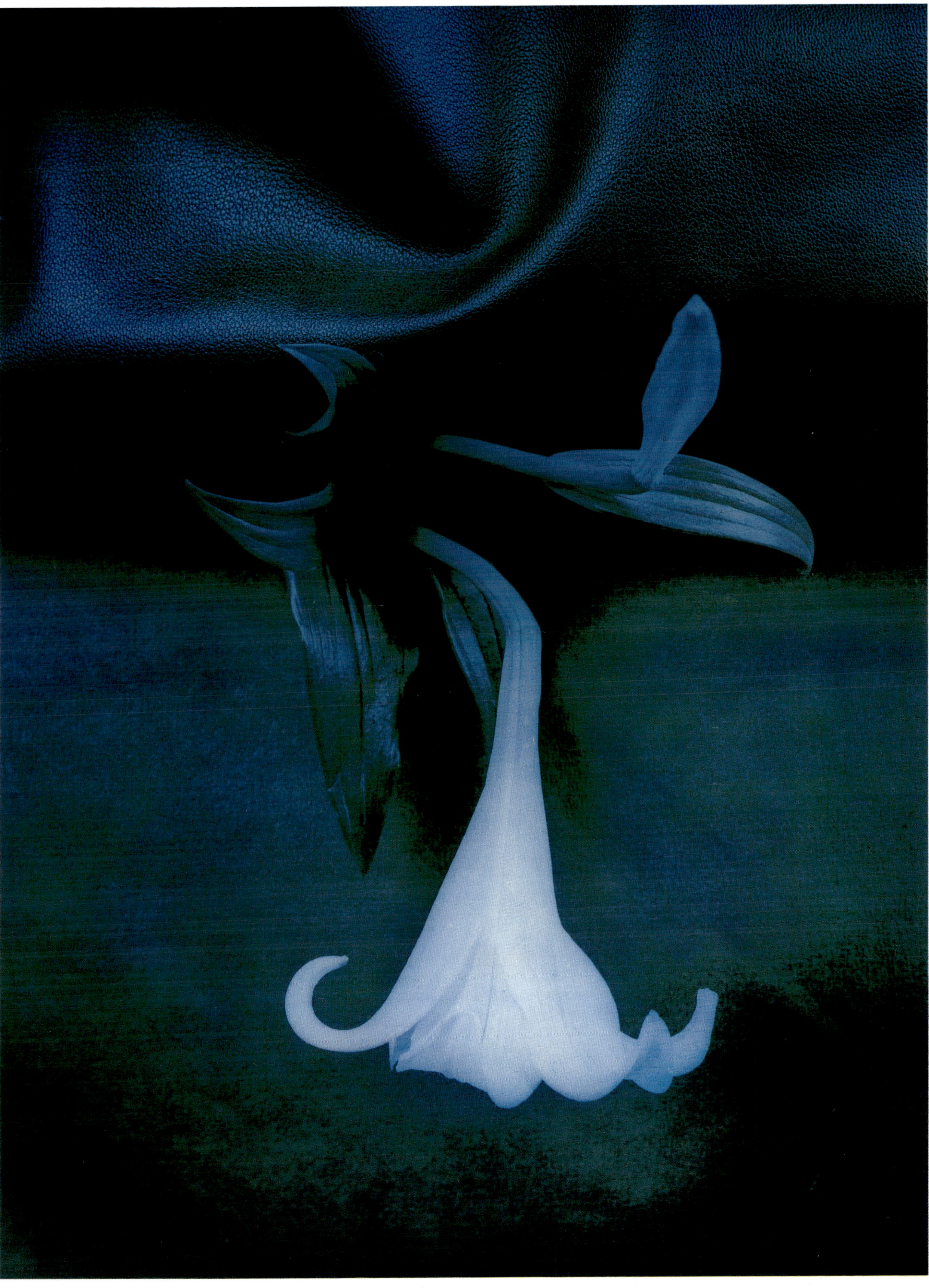

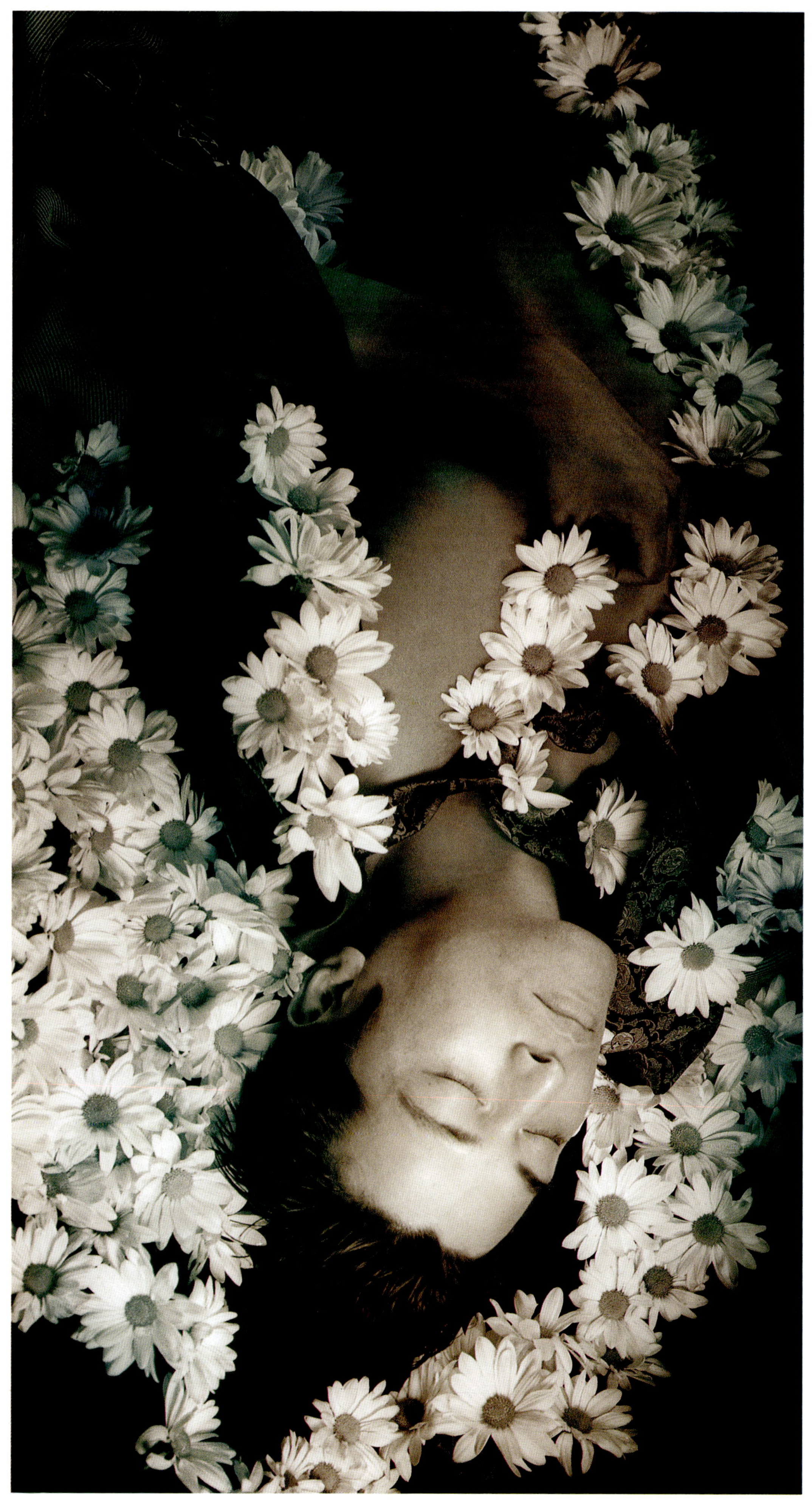

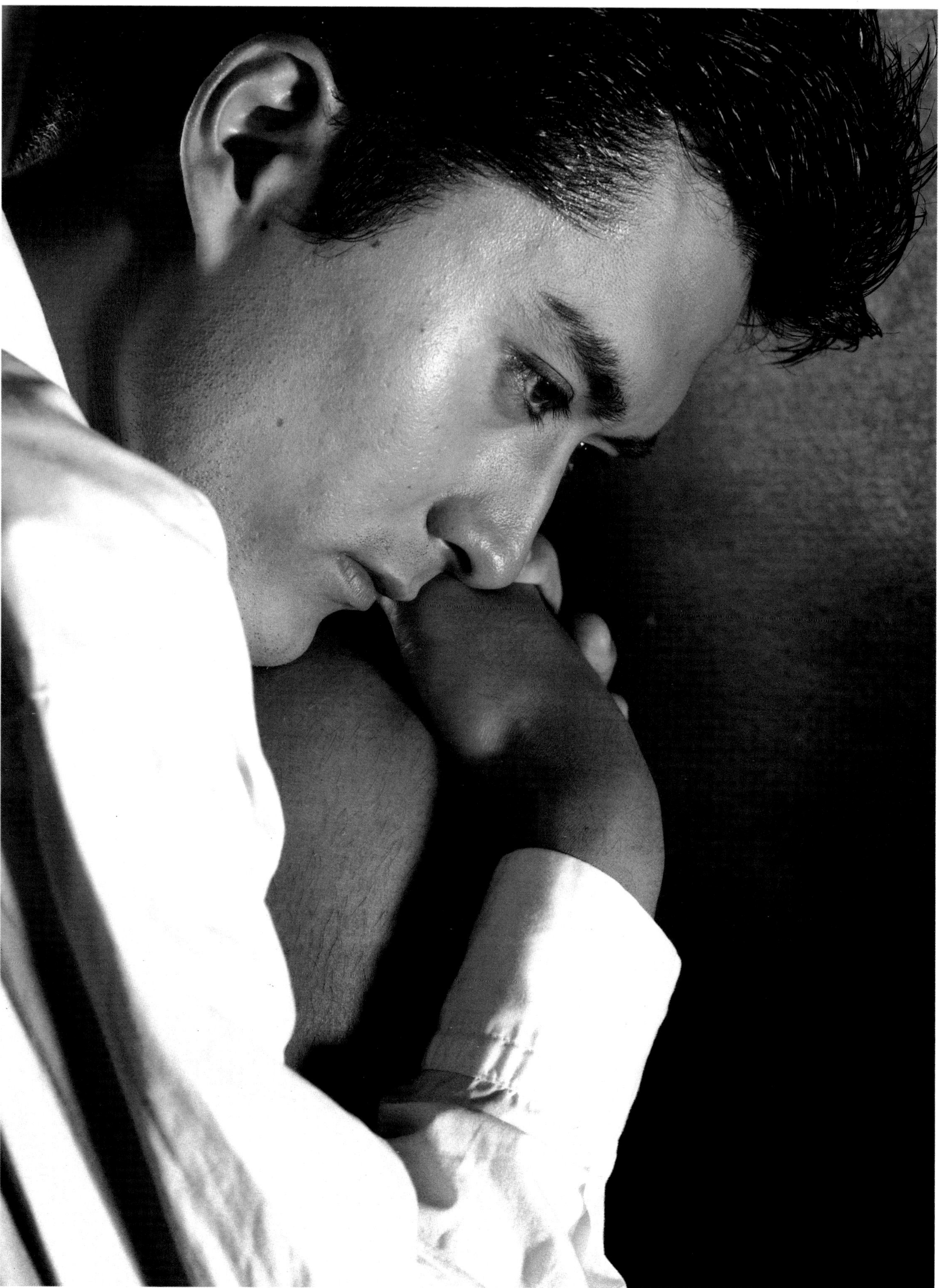

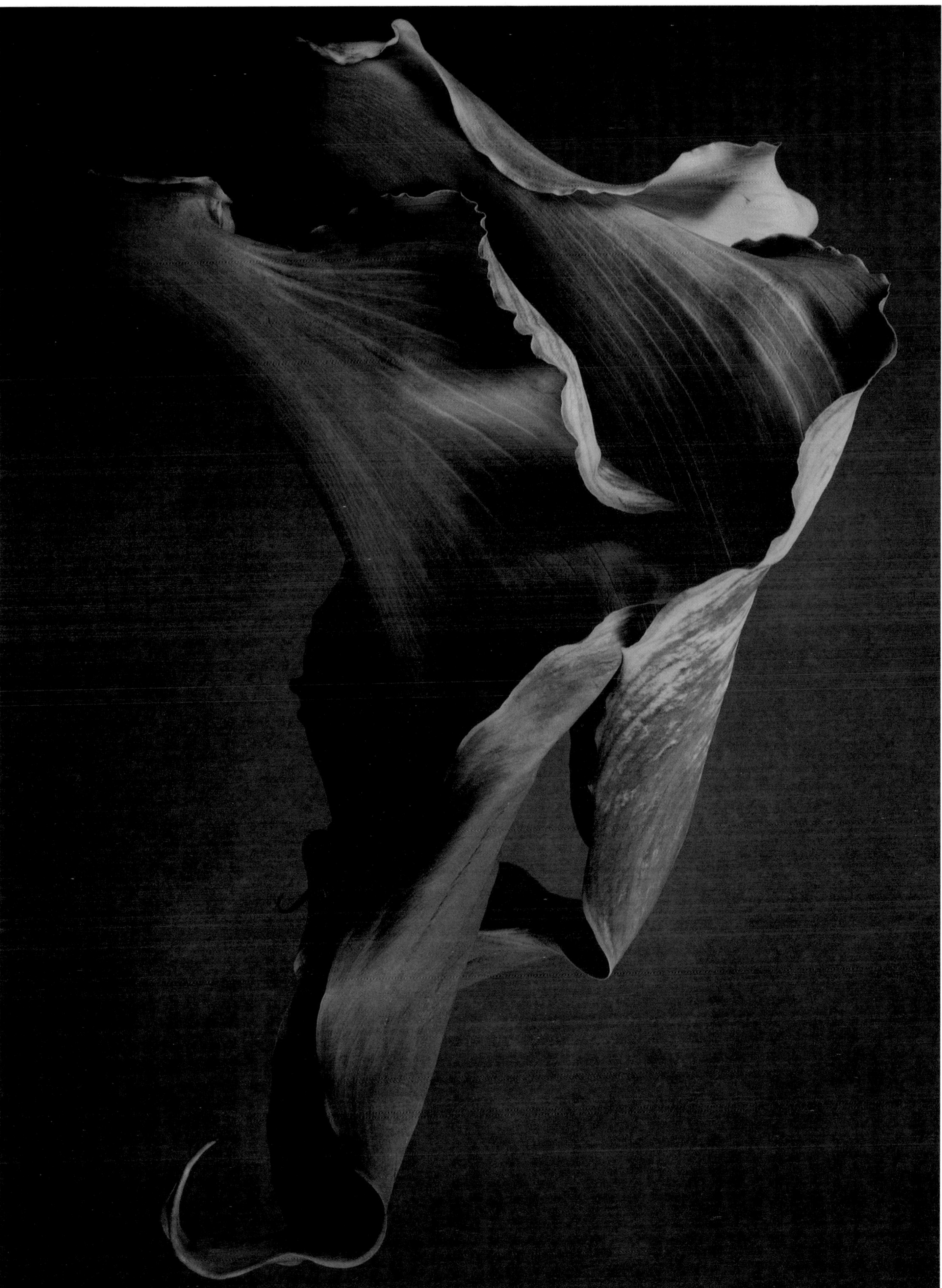

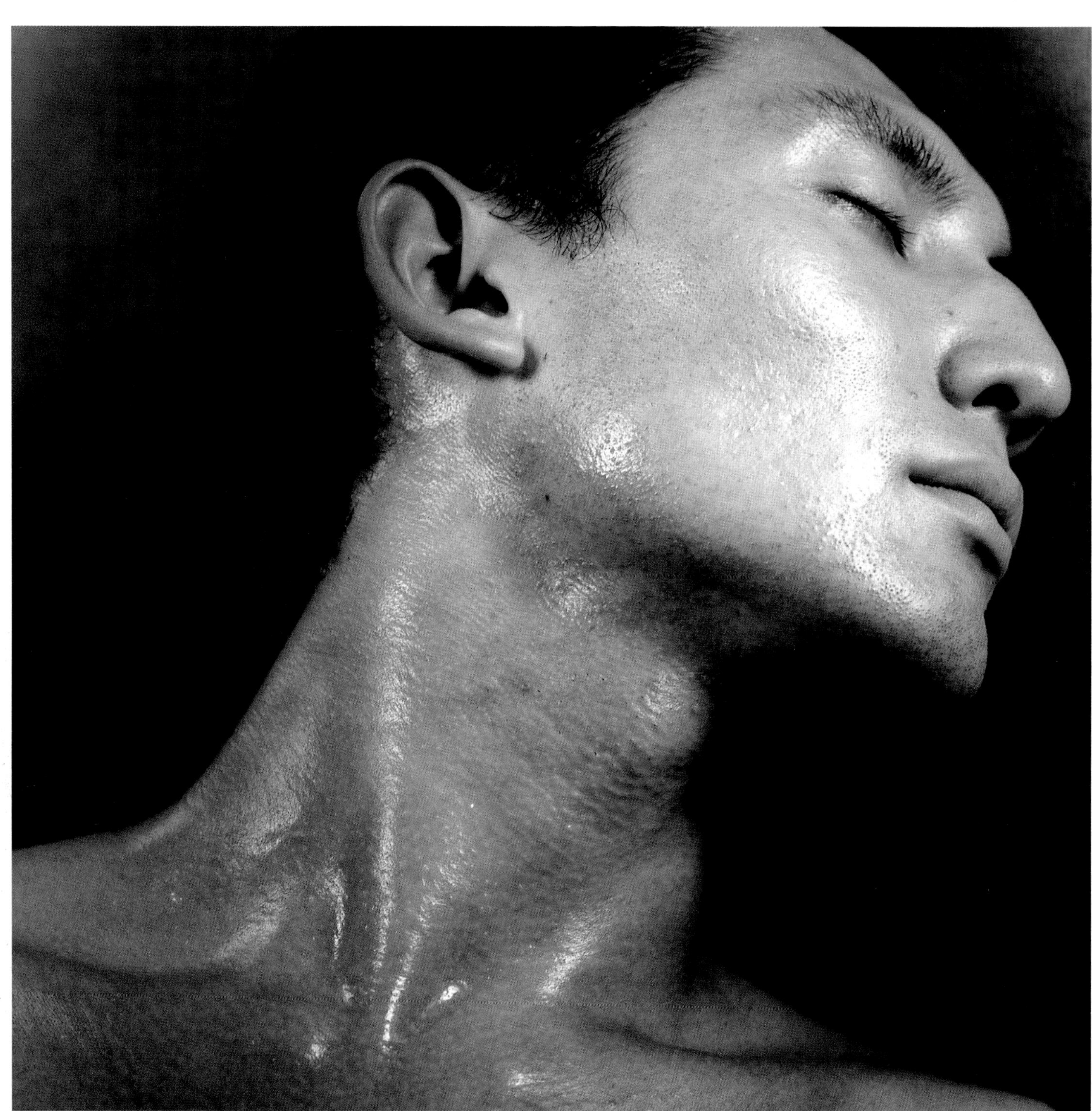

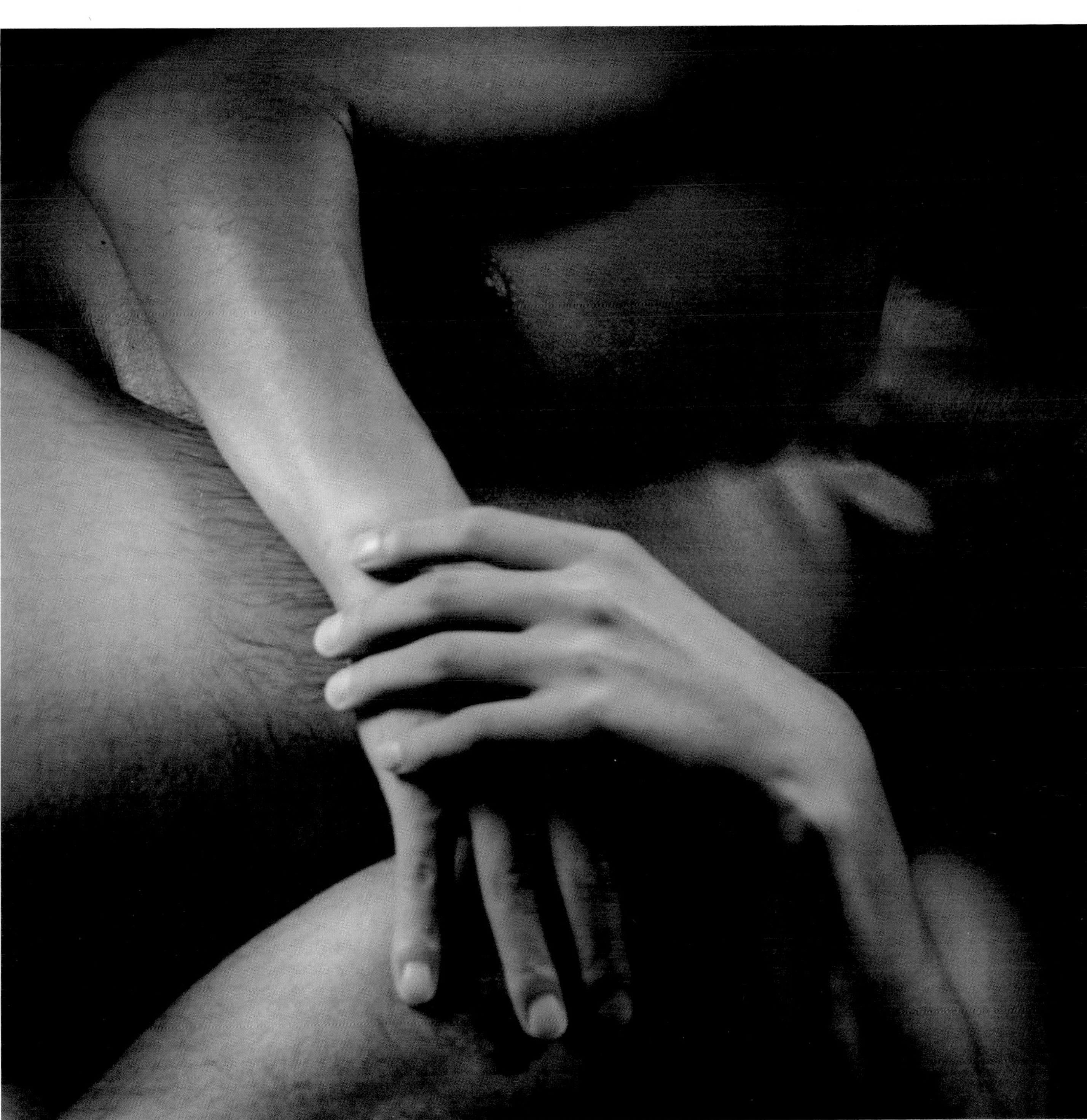

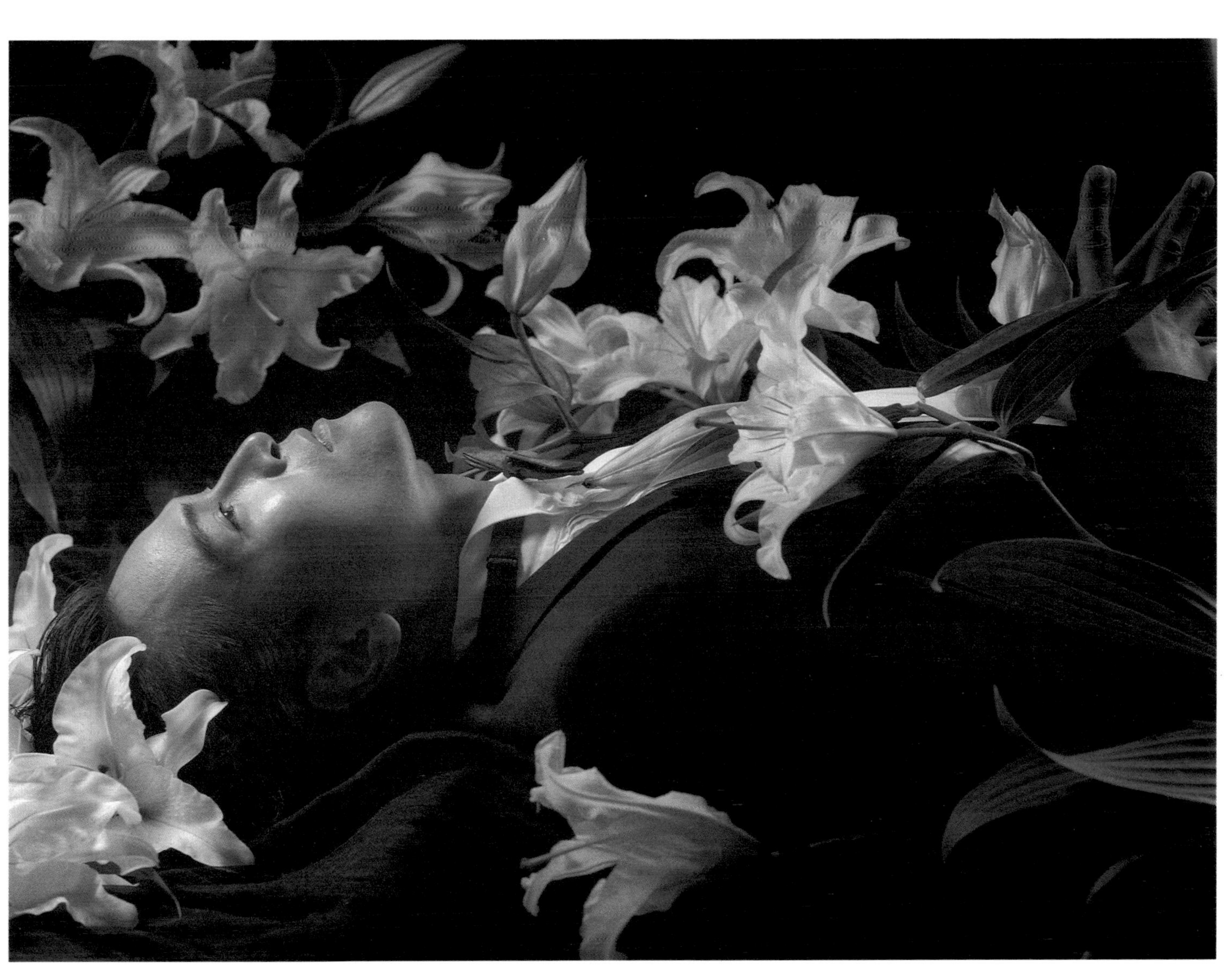

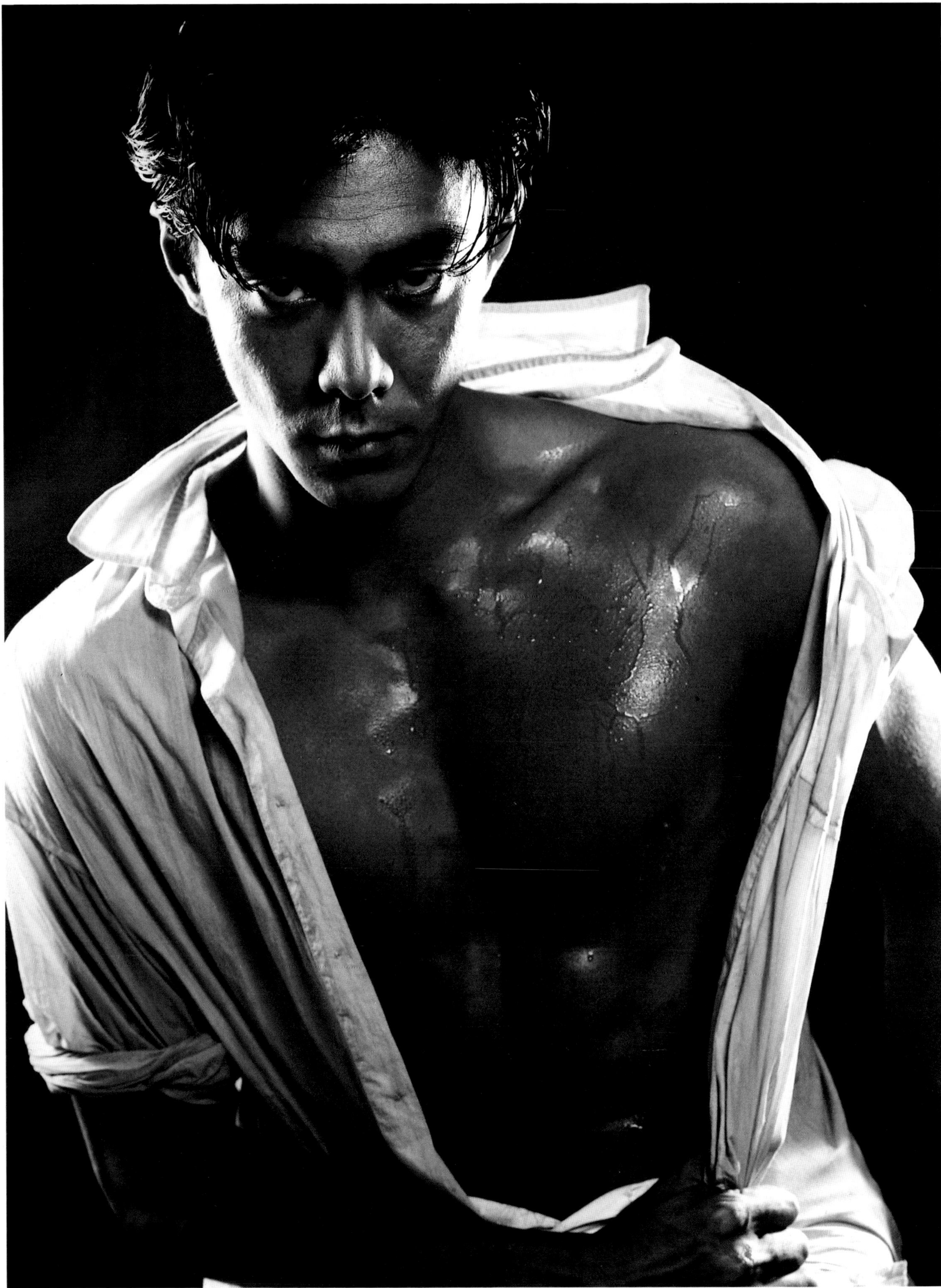

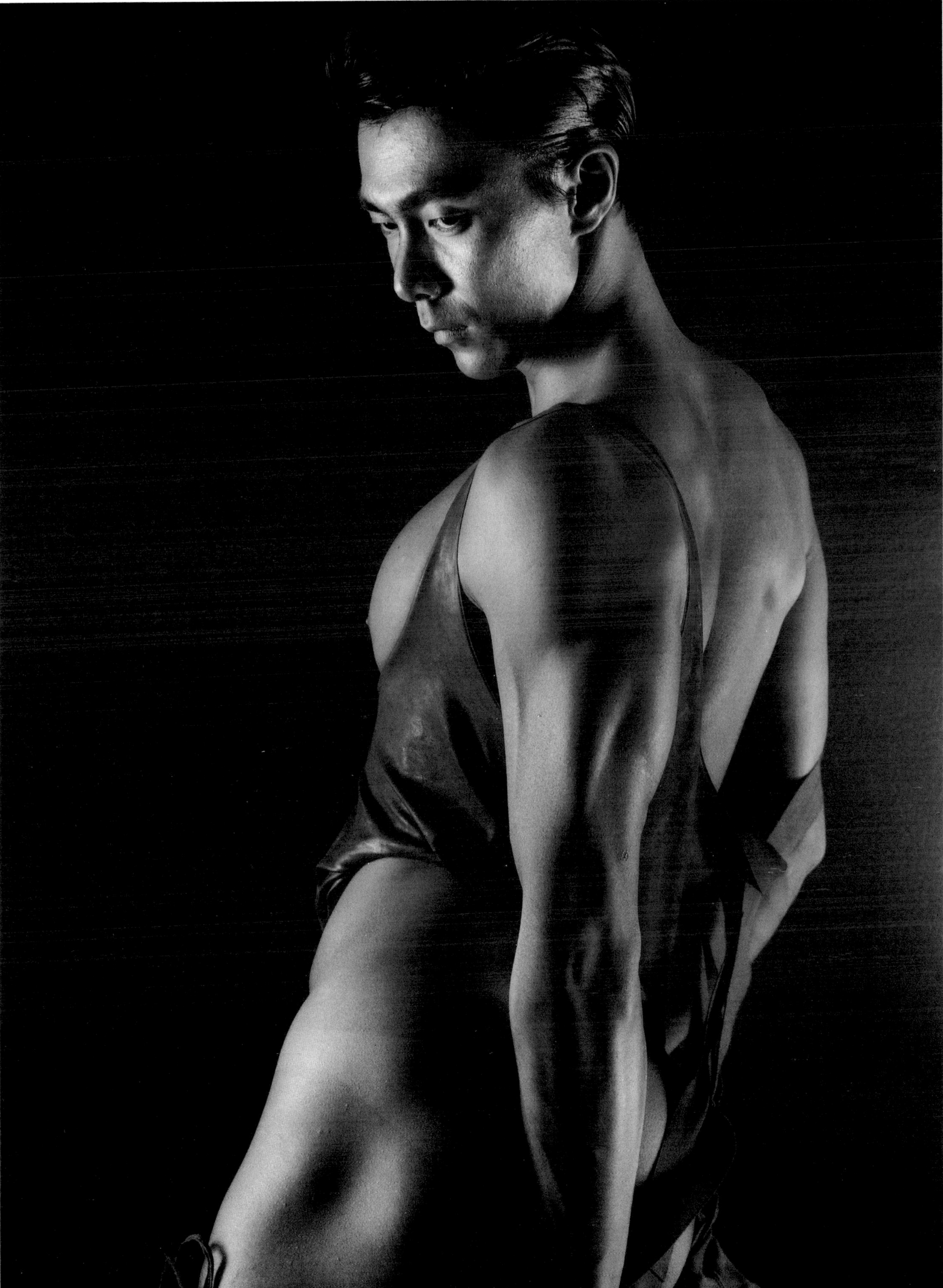

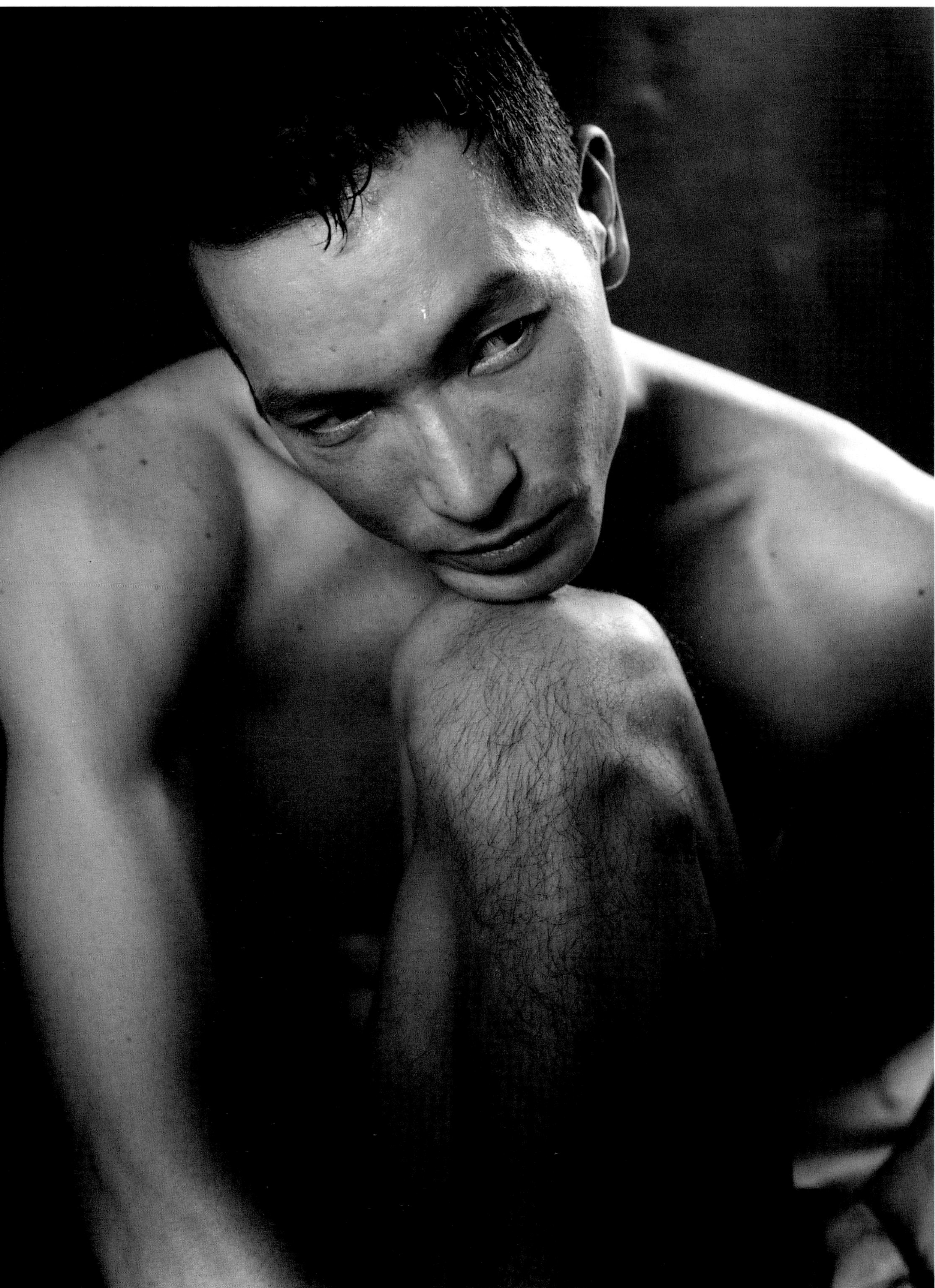

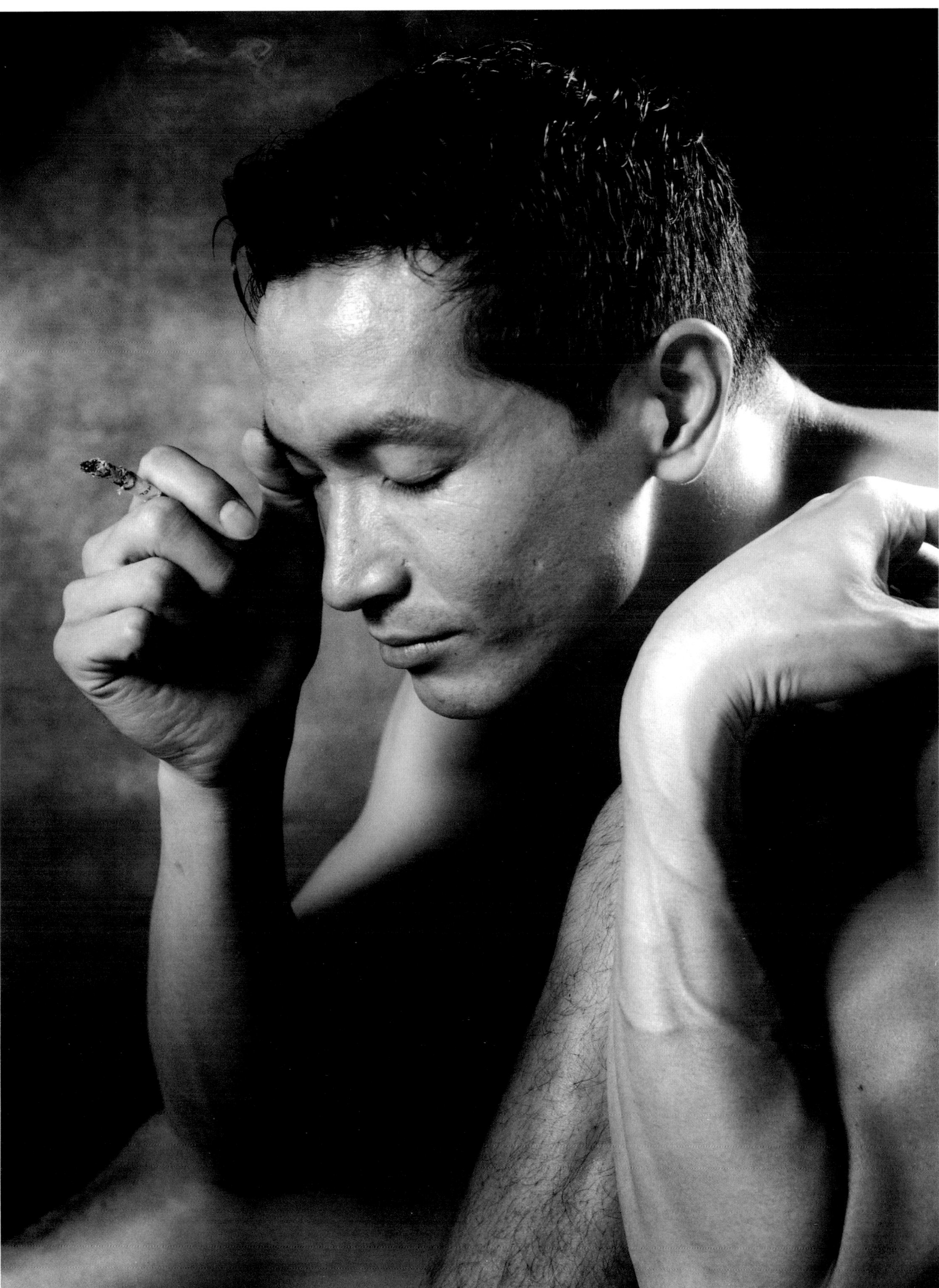

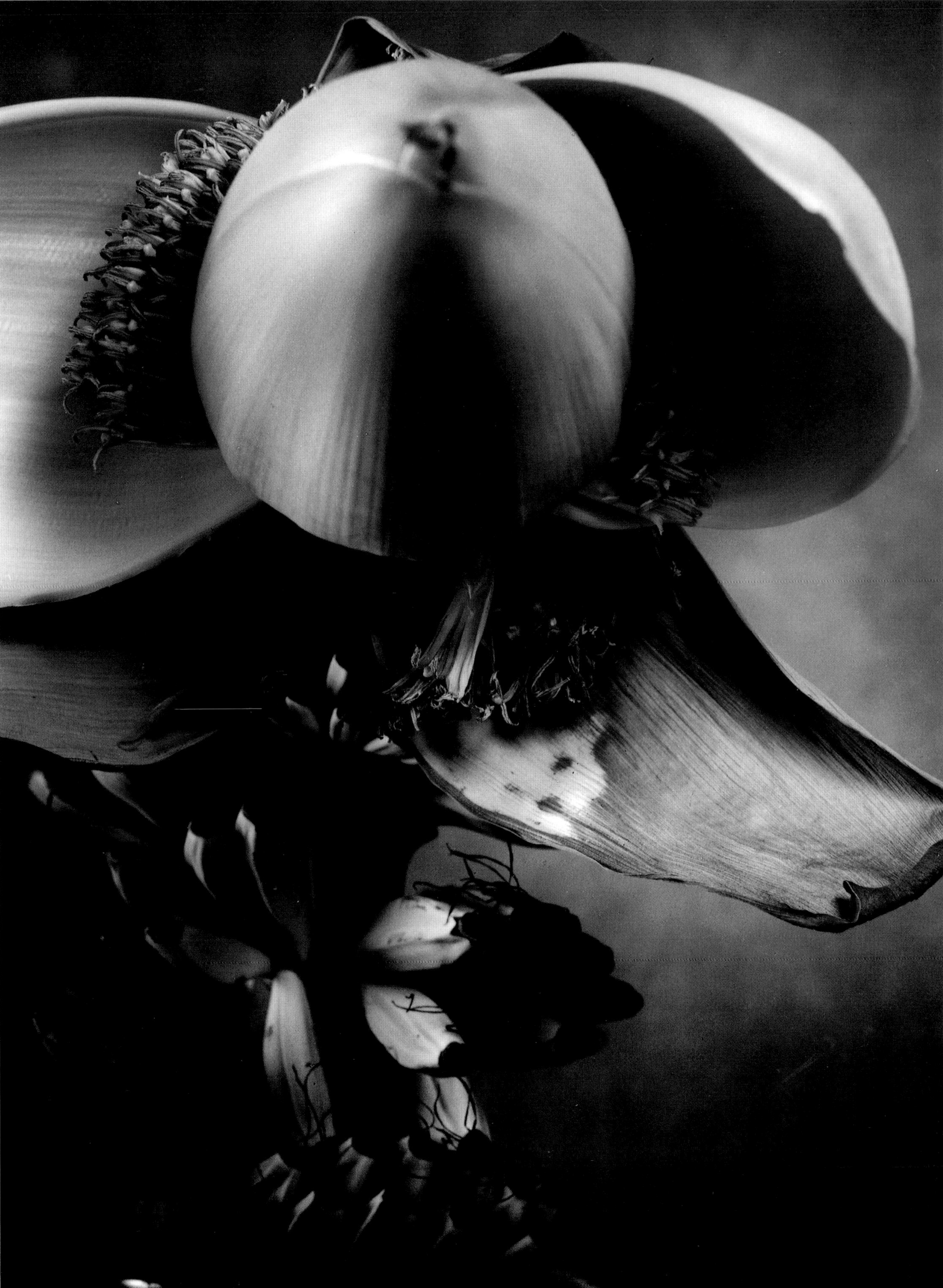

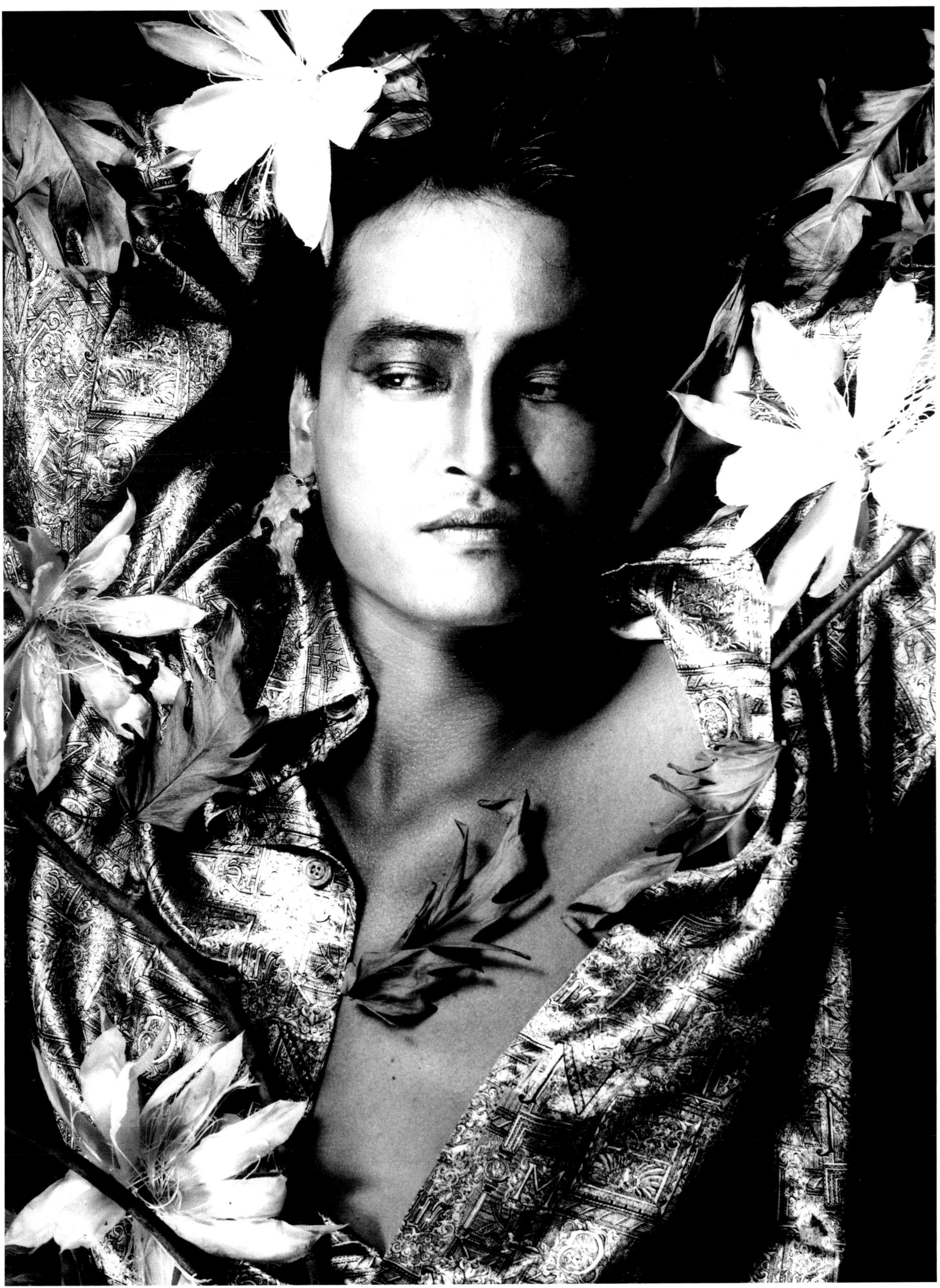

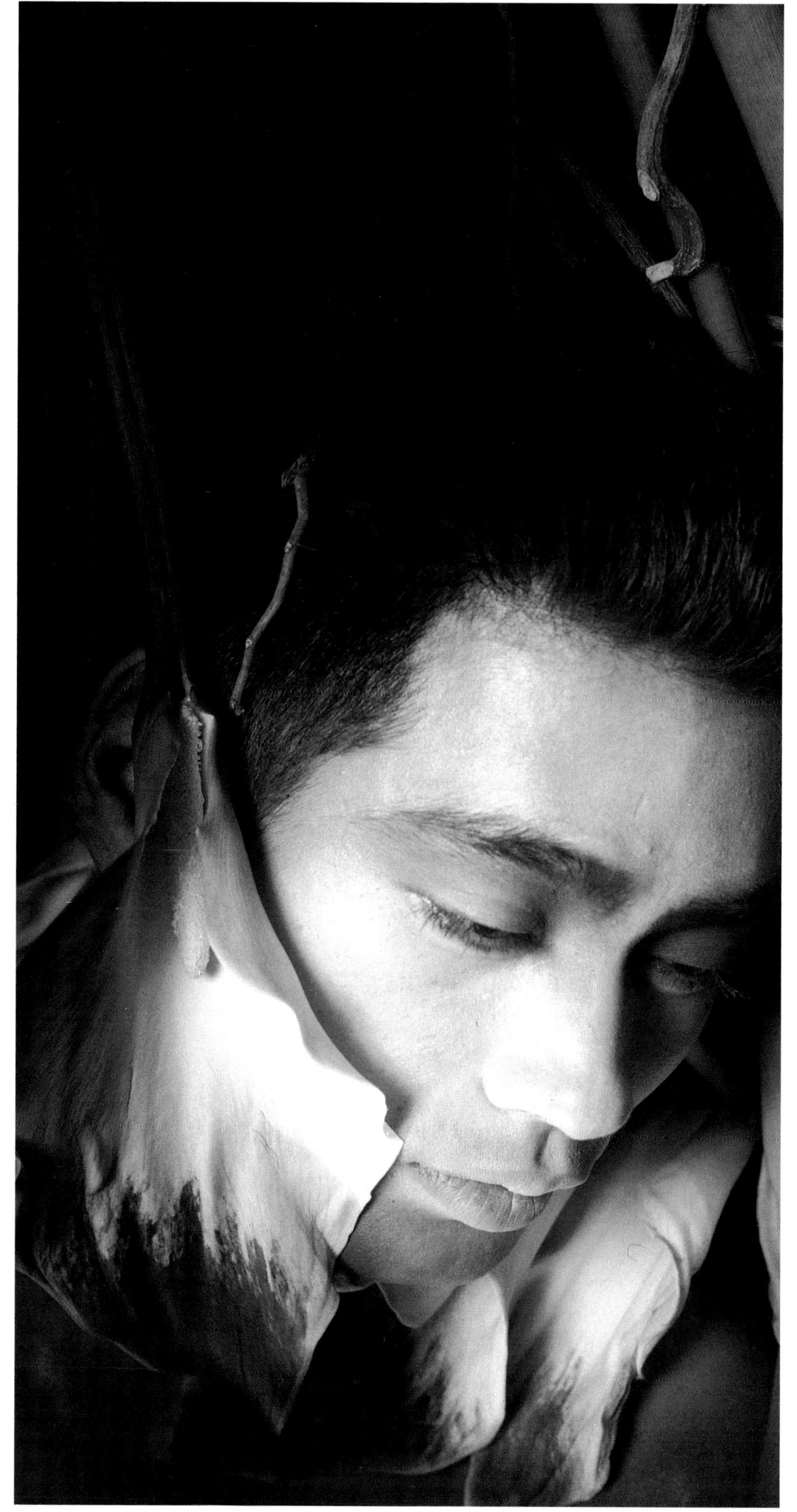

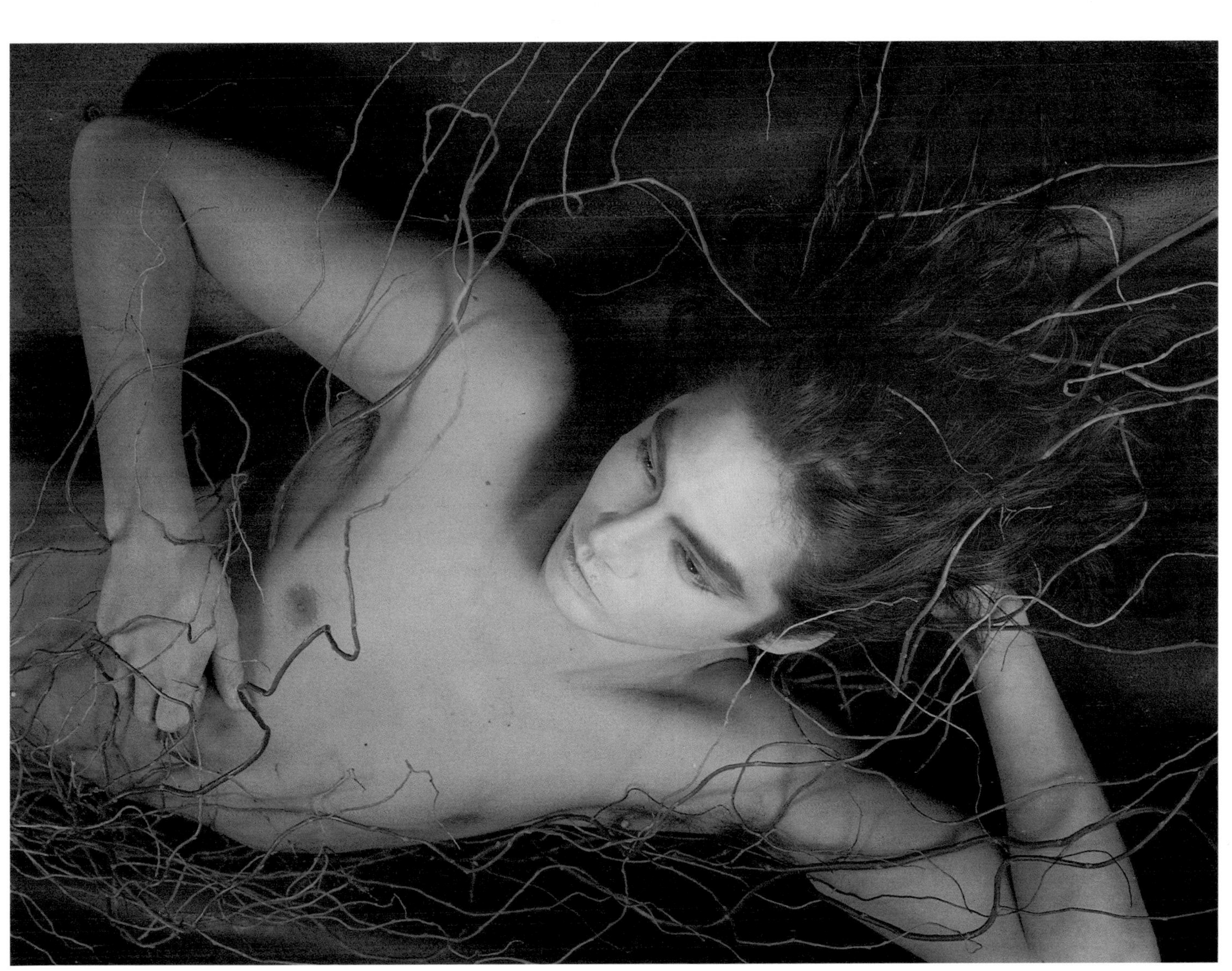

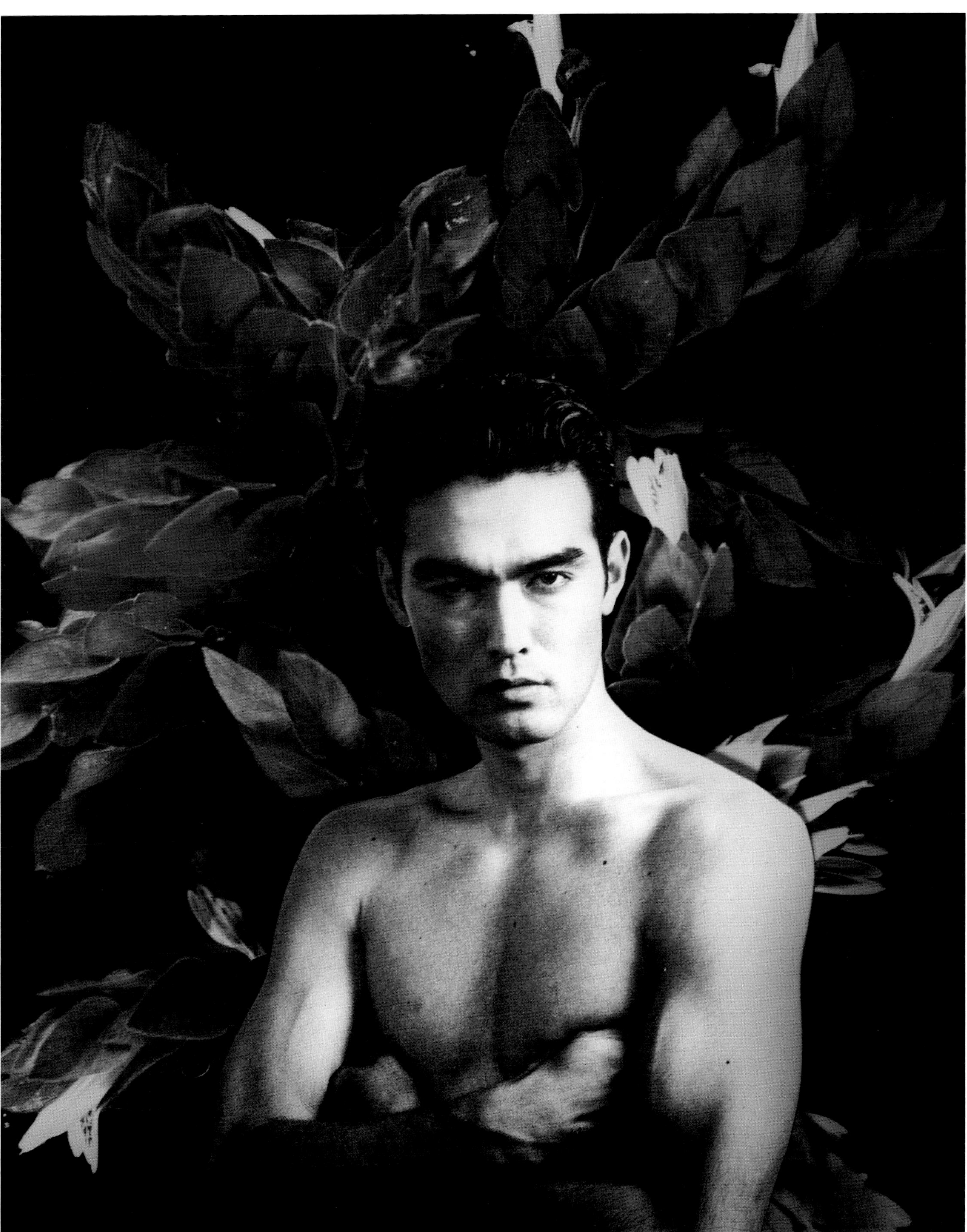

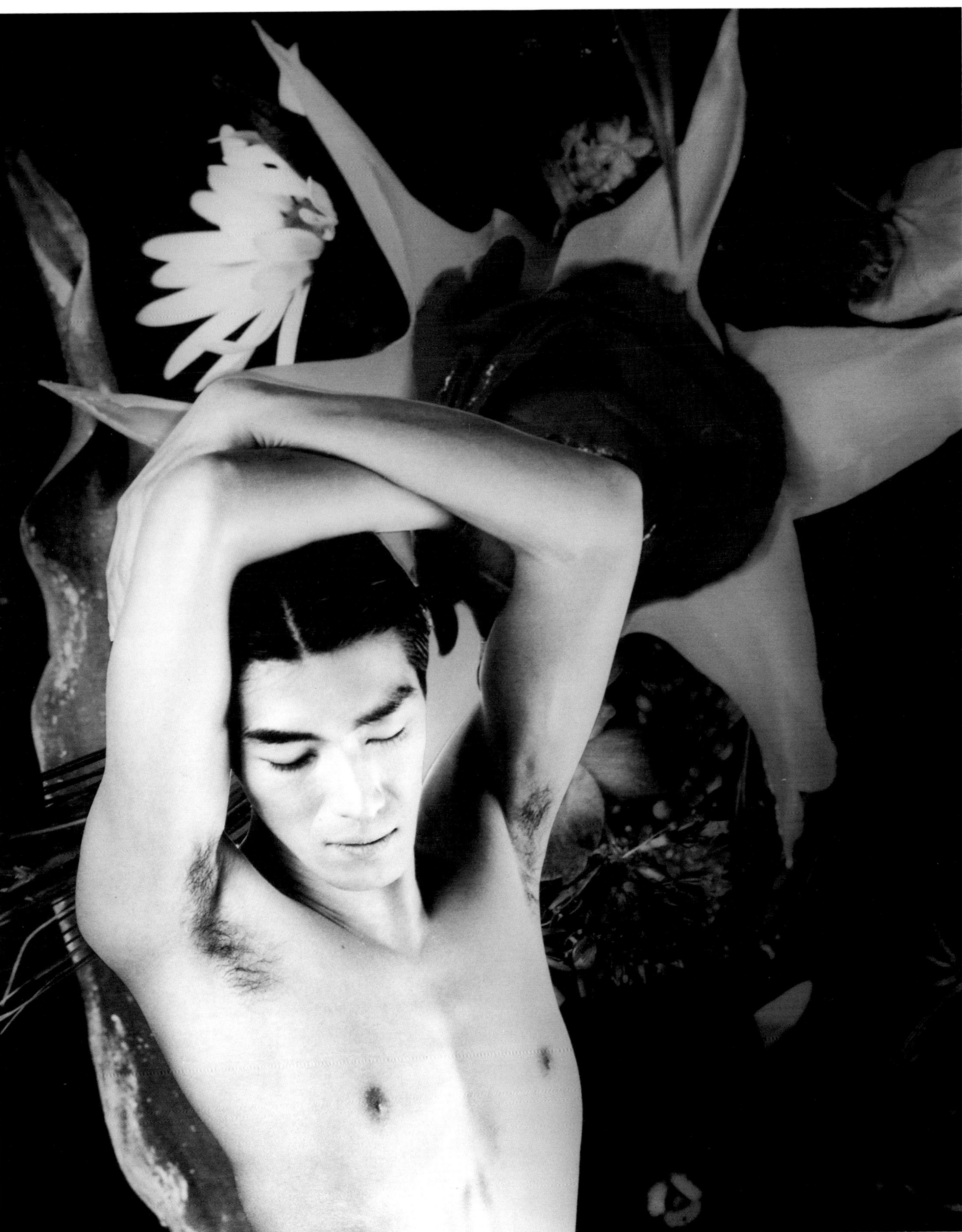

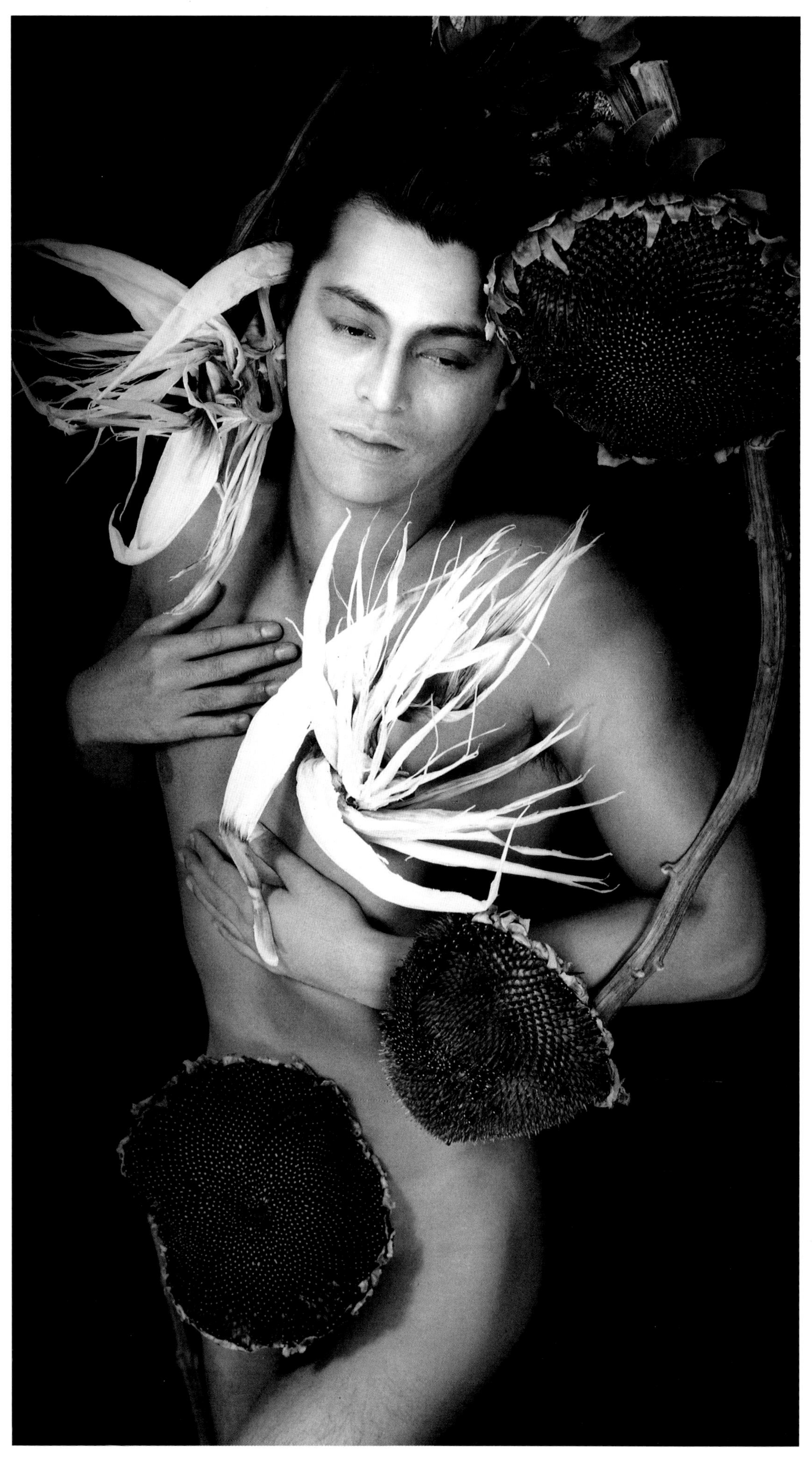

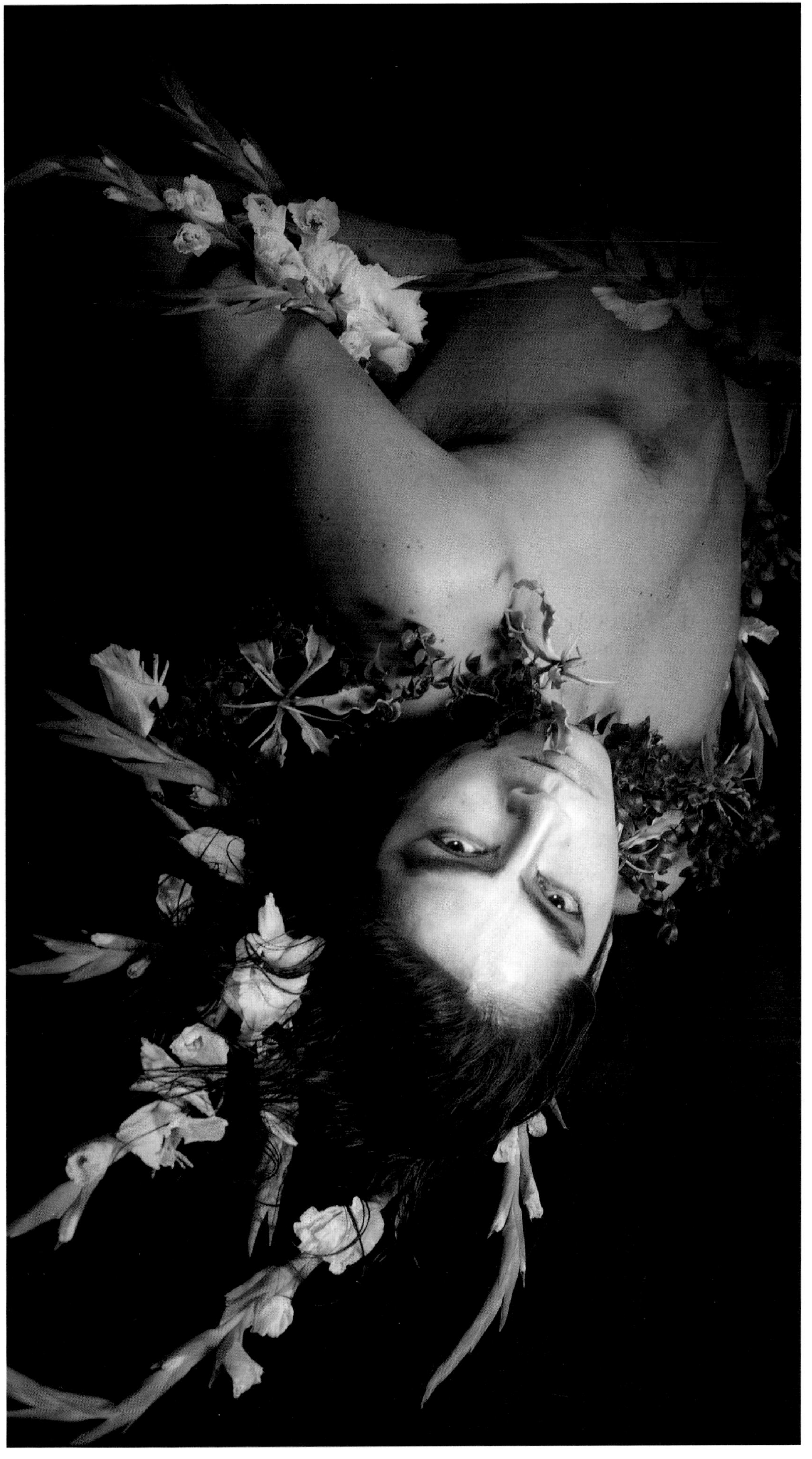

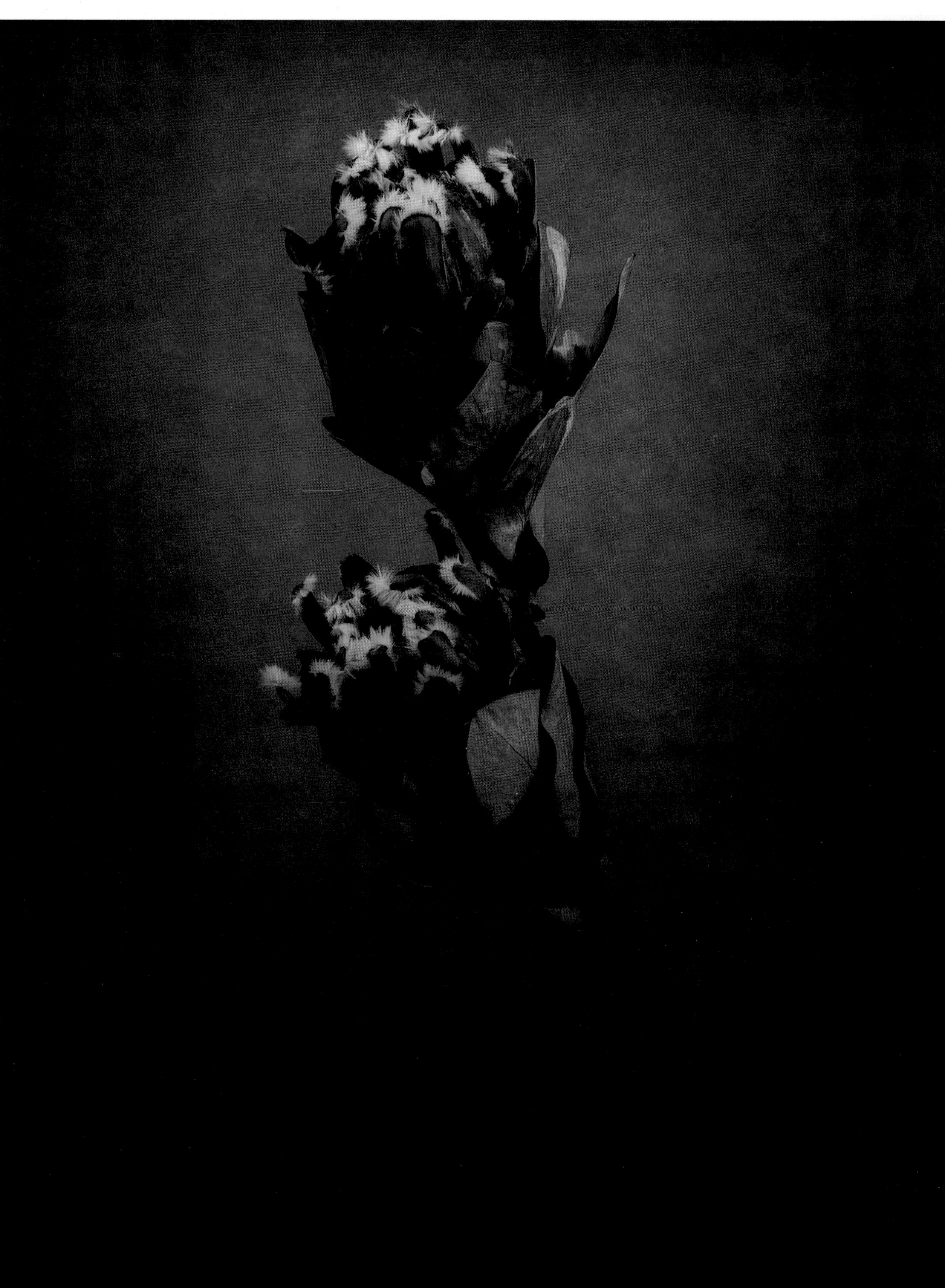

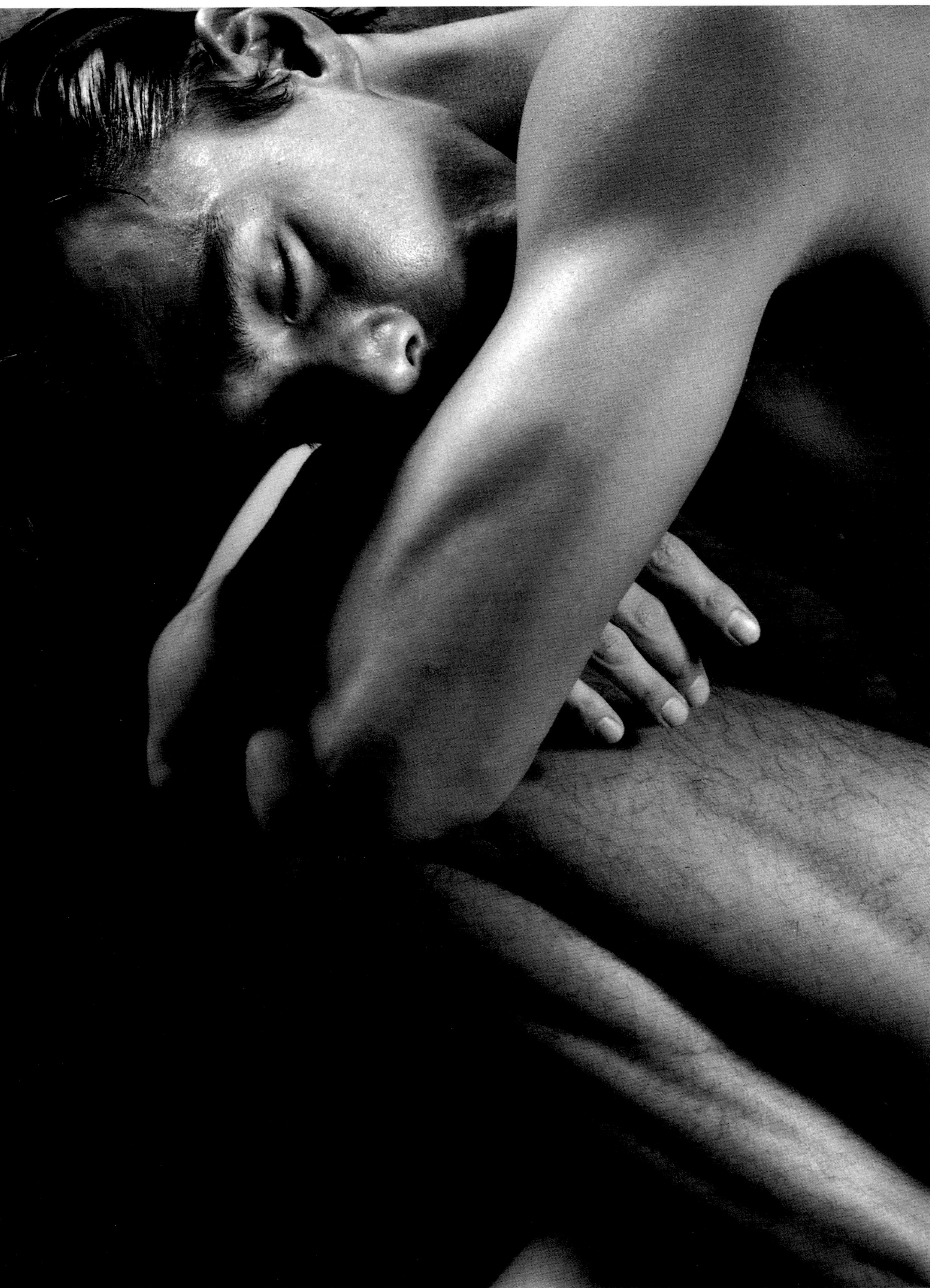

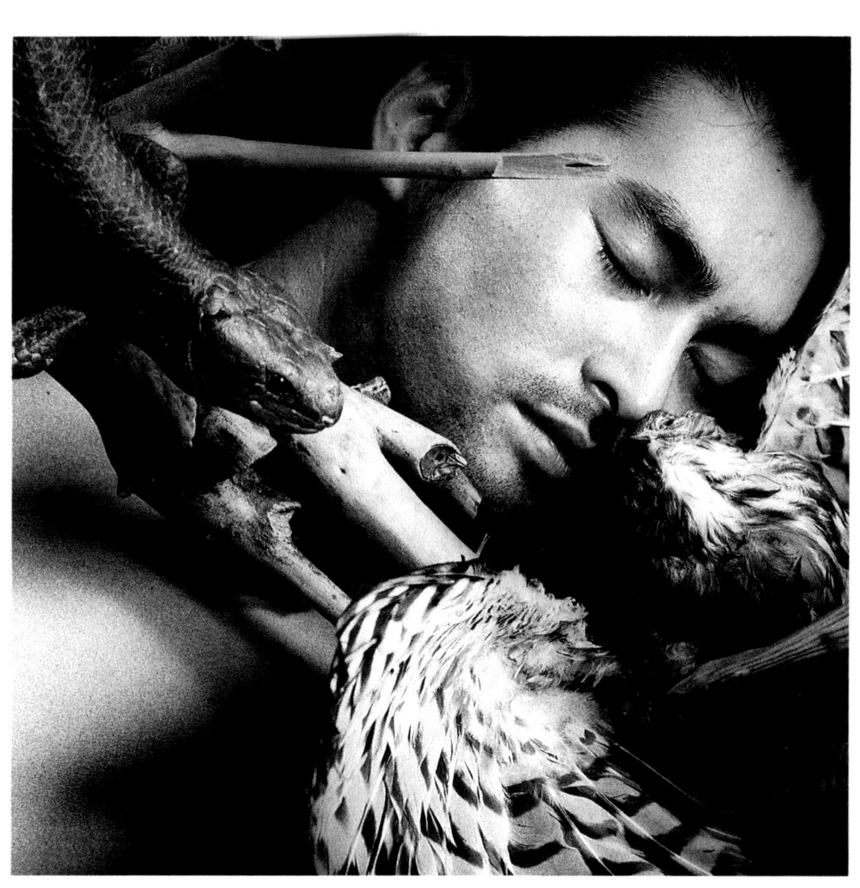

Calcite

Australian Flower	1984	1985	Flex
Yukino	1982	1986	Red Cactus Flowers
Orchid	1984	1989	Trees in Water
Yoshito #101	1983	1988	The Width of a Circle
Mitsuru #203	1988	1984	Lily Magnolia
Tada #504	1990	1989	Doors
Durian	1989	1984	Ren Tamura
Roberte #102	1984	1985	Habotan on Lace of Bruges
Yellow Roses	1986	1983	Bicycle Chain
Untitled #337	1984	1983	Untitled #905
Tatsuya #101	1982	1987	Nepenthes
Tatsuya with Hamayū	1983	1986	Iris
The Flower wrapped by Tulle	1984	1987	Water in Man
Two Tulips	1984	1988	Man holding Cristal Ball
Untitled #502	1983	1988	Man in Tropical Flowers
Untitled #509	1984	1985	Tetsu Takeuchi
Paphiopedilum	1986	1984	White Lily
Tatsuya holding Imitation Frog	1984	1991	Man in Chrysanthmum Flowers
Man holding Chinese Base	1982	1989	Mitsuru Kobori
Untitled #33	1984	1986	Calla Lily
Untitled #303	1984	1990	Eito
Untitled #51	1983	1990	Yasuaki
Tatsuya	1982	1991	Man in White Lily
Roberte	1984	1989	Tetsu #201
Roberte #207	1984	1992	Tetsu #202
Roberte "Mirror Room"	1984	1991	Tatsushi Yamane
Roberte "Stage"	1984	1991	Tatsushi holding a Cigarette
Calla Lily	1984	1990	Flower of Banana
Yoshito	1983	1991	Ken Takagi
Untitled #501	1984	1992	Toshiya Yamamoto
Untitled #804	1982	1992	Toshiya Nagasawa
Habotan	1985	1992	Masanori Gotoh
Untitled #507	1985	1992	Tadafumi Satoh
An Offering	1985	1992	Tatsuro Yanai
Pitu holding Plastics	1988	1992	Toshiya #303
Tetsu "Mirrors"	1990	1984	Australian Flower #503
Ceremony	1989	1991	Tetsu #505
Boild Crab	1984	1992	Man with Corucia Zebrata
Untitled #999	1984		

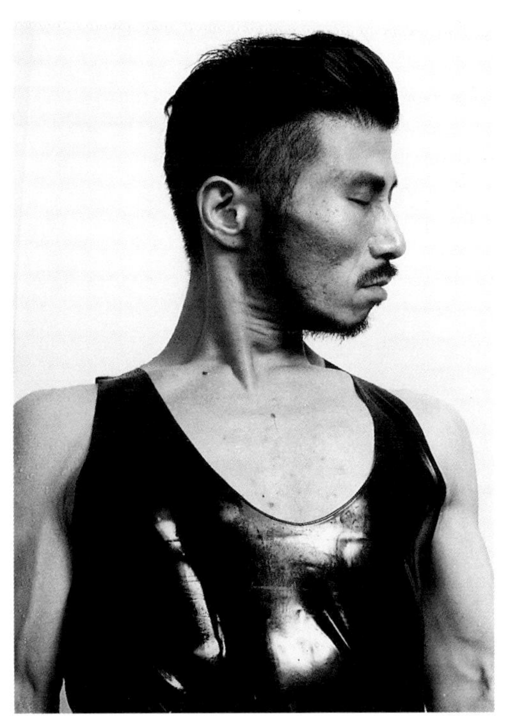

Motoharu Goushi

Ⓒ1993 by Yukiko Tsurutani

Calcite
MOTOHARU GOUSHI

First Edition Apr. 20 1993
Editing:Shuhei Takahashi
Co-Editing:Ken Kawai
Book Design:Yasushi Fujimoto, Hideki Minami+Cap
English Translation:Kazuko Behrens

Publisher:Taro Kaneda
Published by Treville Co.,Ltd.
203, 2-11-17, Shoto Shibuya-ku, Tokyo, zip150/Phone 03(3481)5611
Distributed by Libro Port Co.,Ltd.
2-23-2, Minami-Ikebukuro Toshima-ku, Tokyo, zip171/Phone 03(3983)6191
Printed and bound by Toppan Printing Co.,Ltd.

カルサイト ［方解石］
郷司基晴

初版発行/1993月4月20日
編集/高橋周平
共同編集/川合健一
ブック・デザイン/藤本やすし、南 英樹＋キャップ
翻訳/カズコ・ベアレンツ

発行者/金田太郎
発行/株式会社トレヴィル
東京都渋谷区松濤2-11-17-203 〒150 Phone 03(3481)5611
発売/株式会社リブロポート
東京都豊島区南池袋2-23-2 〒171 Phone 03(3983)6191
印刷製本/凸版印刷株式会社

乱丁落丁本はお取り替えいたします。

ISBN4-8457-0734-9 C0072

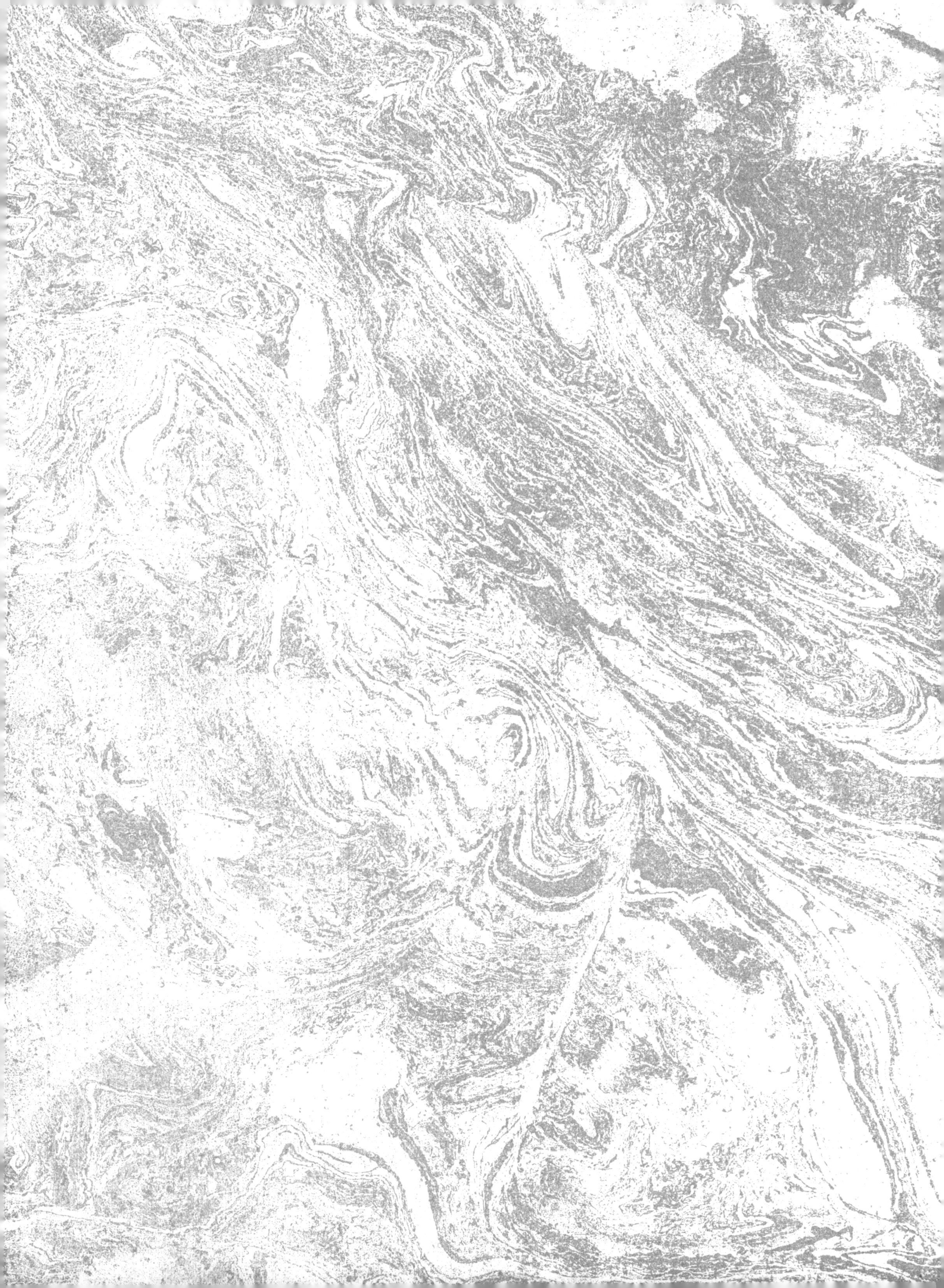

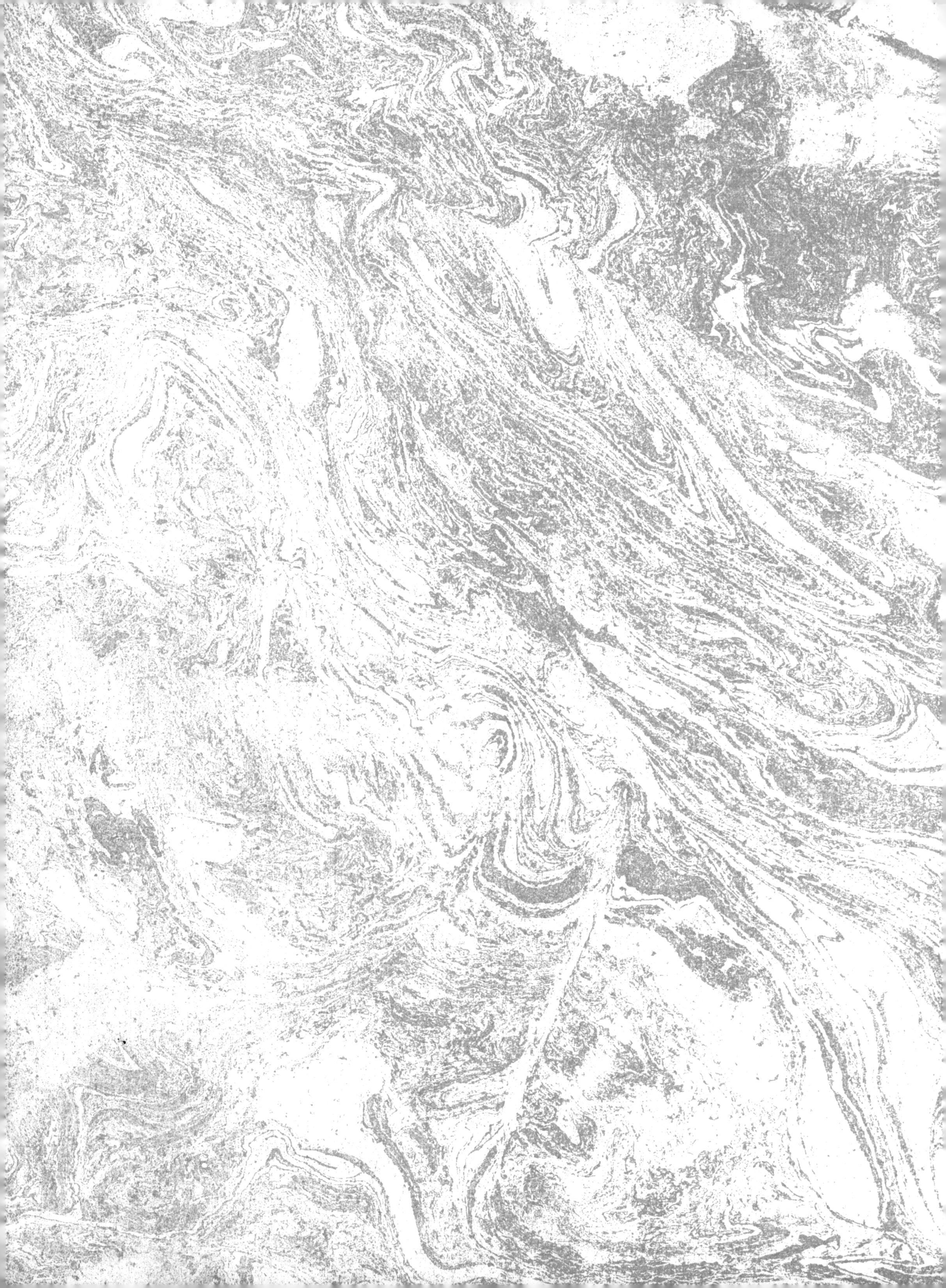